Pleiadian Activation of Ou

CW01498806

"This extraordinary book by Pavlir
present crazy times. It not only provides a completely new perspective
on what is happening on Earth right now but also shares support for
dealing with this on a higher frequency and thus staying anchored
in the light."

— SARAH JASMIN CARTSBURG, the Multidimensional Medium,
author, and manifestation expert

"Pavlina Klemm shares Pleiadian messages that guide you through
the shift into higher dimensions. You will learn about the healing
power of the Sun, the activation of your pineal gland, and ways to
free your soul from old energetic programs. Channeled wisdom,
affirmations, and exercises open the door to self-love and cosmic
freedom, while messages from Atlanteans, inner-Earth civilizations,
and cosmic children remind you of your divine origin and the unique
time of transformation we are living in now."

— MONIKA CARDINAL, author, speaker,
and channel of higher consciousness

"Pavlina Klemm's *Pleiadian Activation of Our Sacred Heart Space*
is an illuminating book, infused with the frequency of love. It was
such a pleasure to meet her wise Pleiadian friends—Orella, Vilalata,
Ramuel, Wahou, Milin, and Orin—who share profound insights
about living in a 5D heart-centered space. They reveal how 3D and
5D exist in parallel and how we can choose to connect with higher
dimensions, universes, and beings of light. I was especially fascinated
to learn that Ra is the soul of the Sun—constantly transmitting light
and positive thoughts to us—as well as the importance of activating
the pineal gland to communicate with other worlds."

— FRANZISKA SIRAGUSA, principal teacher with the
Diana Cooper School of White Light and author of
Feng Shui with Archangels, Unicorns, and Dragons

"In times of great transformation, it is especially important to listen to our hearts. This book by Pavlina Klemm welcomes you into the space of your soul, the space within where everything can be transformed. Through the Pleiadians, Pavlina connects us to the high cosmic vibrations and dimensions of the heart and soul level. Experience a cosmic activation of your sacred heart space through the powerful presence of the Pleiadians at your side. Let Pavlina's incomparable words of love touch you and guide you on your path with light. This book will enrich your life, as it has mine, in wonderful ways; you will surely feel the positive changes immediately, just as I did."

— MELANIE MISSING, creator of unicorn essences and author on unicorns, angels, and Avalon

PLEIADIAN
ACTIVATION OF OUR
SACRED HEART SPACE

LIBERATING THE HUMAN SOUL

Pavlina Klemm

Translated by
Hilary Snellgrove

FINDHORN PRESS

Findhorn Press
One Park Street
Rochester, Vermont 05767
www.findhornpress.com

Findhorn Press is a division of Inner Traditions International

© 2022, 2025 by Pavlina Klemm
German edition © 2023 by AMRA Verlag & Records
English edition © 2025 by Findhorn Press

Originally published in German in 2023 by AMRA Verlag & Records as
Lichtbotschaften von den Plejaden 9: Erwachen im Licht der Freiheit

All rights reserved. No part of this book may be reproduced or utilized in any form
or by any means, electronic or mechanical, including photocopying, recording, or by
any information storage and retrieval system, without permission in writing from the
publisher. No part of this book may be used or reproduced to train artificial intelligence
technologies or systems.

Disclaimer
The information in this book is given in good faith and intended for information
only. Neither author nor publisher can be held liable by any person for any loss
or damage whatsoever which may arise from the use of this book or any of the
information therein.

Cataloging-in-Publication data for this title is available from the Library of Congress

ISBN 979-1-88850-319-5 (print)
ISBN 979-1-88850-320-1 (ebook)

Printed and bound in the United States by Lake Book Manufacturing, LLC

10 9 8 7 6 5 4 3 2 1

Edited by Jacqui Lewis
Cover and interior illustrations by Josephine Wall, www.josephinewall.co.uk
Text design and layout by Damian Keenan
This book was typeset in Adobe Garamond Pro, Calluna Sans, and with
ITC Century Std used as a display typeface.

To send correspondence to the author of this book, mail a first-class letter to the author
c/o Inner Traditions, One Park Street, Rochester, VT 05767, USA and we will forward
the communication, or contact the author directly at **https://pavlina-klemm.com**.

For All Beings Who Have
Made Up Their Minds to Enter
Their Own Sacred Heart Space
of Freedom.

With love
Pavlina

Contents

PART TWO
Messages from the Pleiadians for
the Changing of the Time

APPENDICES

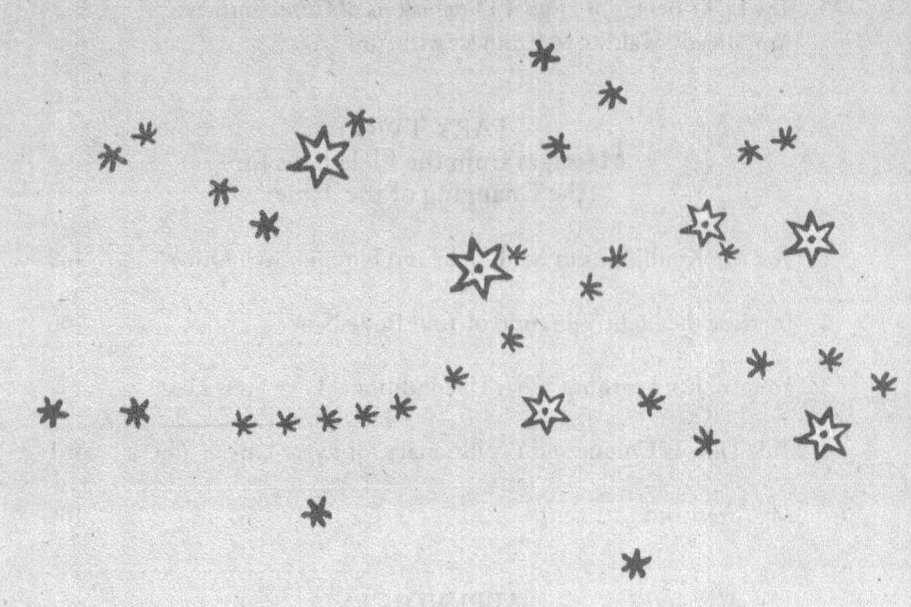

Preface

Dear reader of these light-filled messages!

I would like to share with you my great joy in being able to enter your world of thoughts and connect with the light of your soul through the book you are holding in your hands.

Before I start a new book, the first thing I do is go to a stationery shop. I have loved the smell of paper and books from an early age. Once there, I intuitively allow myself to be inspired in choosing a new notebook for writing down the messages of the Pleiadian beings. The individual manuscript notebooks I use for writing my books all have different colors and motifs. For this book, I chose a pink-colored cover with a silver edge.

And when I started communicating with the Pleiadians and receiving their messages and exercises for the new book, they immediately told me that this book would be all about love and the possibilities that love with its special frequency gives us. I immediately realized why a pink-colored notebook had been exactly the right choice. ☺ ☺

The frequency of love runs through this wonderful new book from beginning to end. As the Pleiadians never tire of telling us, love is the strongest positive frequency and a force that can heal everything. Love heals us and love guides us toward the liberation of our human soul—what an important motto for this time!

Once again, the Pleiadians accompany us "step by step," helping us to heal, to understand, and to find light and freedom in our souls. Once more, they have provided us with much information that enables us to understand our own nature and the essence of the world around us. They help us to discover everything of importance on our own so that we no longer have to ask others or search elsewhere for answers but can trust in ourselves.

I am particularly pleased to say that we will also be hearing from Vilalata, the wise young Pleiadian from *Pleiadian Soul Healing*. She will be guiding us through her information with the express intention of teaching us how to channel and communicate with light beings. She will be helping us to rid ourselves of the fear that binds our hearts and prevents us from loving ourselves and communicating with the world of light. The energies that Vilalata transmits through her words are wonderfully warming and charged with immeasurable love. Her whole being is synonymous with love. She is so often in the angelic worlds that she radiates angelic love.

I have no less love for the energy of Orella, which has accompanied me for many years in my earthly incarnation. She is the oldest member of the Pleiadian group that communicates with me. Her theme is "heart healing," which she teaches us with infinite love, wisdom, and understanding.

Orella and Vilalata are in regular contact with me when I am writing my books. They often accompany me during my seminars and my training courses for healers-to-be. When they decide to enter our time period, they bring so much love with them that seminar participants are able to immediately remember and feel the love of their divine home. This provides an opportunity for an individual's inner child to heal spontaneously and for various negative issues to leave their reality once and for all.

I have noticed that the light vibration of our cells increases instantly when Orella and Vilalata enter our time period together, because the love that emanates from these two beings makes even the smallest particles of our body vibrate with light. The healing of various aspects then happens automatically as a "side effect" because the strong vibration of this love allows lower frequencies and elements to leave without much ado.

I have also noticed that, when the frequency of love enters our time period, there is a light-filled expansion of the consciousness of the participants. Their consciousness connects with their higher consciousness and their higher intelligence. And their higher consciousness connects them with all the light beings that pertain to them and accompany them. As a result, these participants make huge quantum leaps in their spiritual development. And that all happens automatically, without any effort.

Love heals, regenerates, and liberates, and it brings us back to our original divine order. I was able to observe this on several occasions when I met up again, some time later, with a seminar group that had been in contact with the frequency of love that Pleiadian and luminous beings had brought them. Each time I met them, I noticed that the energy of the whole group had increased significantly.

But, of course, it is not just Orella and Vilalata who enter our time period. The Pleiadian group, which faithfully accompanies me and provides me with a great deal of information, naturally includes other helpful members. In *Pleiadian Soul Healing*, they introduced themselves individually for the first time, giving us a precise understanding of who is actually working with us.

Ramuel is a Pleiadian healer who supports us through any healing process. He gives us exercises that help us to heal. Wahou is also a Pleiadian healer who programs number sequences and symbols for us energetically and passes them on. Milin gives us information about the development of the human community. Rahul informs us about the physical and energetic state of our planet. His wife, Arilla, is a great help to him in that respect. And when something important comes up concerning the overall development or state of humanity, planet Earth, or other galactic processes, I have the honor of speaking with Orin, who is the highest member of the Cosmic Council.

This Pleiadian group, which is in the seventh dimension of consciousness, works with Pleiadian beings of the ninth dimension of consciousness. The Pleiadian beings of the ninth level of consciousness have no physical body. They have already come so close to the light in their development that they are in direct contact with it. Their bodies are of a light-filled, crystalline nature.

They no longer recognize boundaries between spaces, dimensions, or times because their subtle, luminous bodies enable them to enter the most diverse realms.

There are, of course, countless light beings who work together with the Pleiadians and Pleiadian light beings and help to transfer the information to my books. The communication that takes place between the Pleiadians and the light beings is full of love and harmonious cooperation. All together, these beings provide us with their information and healing frequencies in the purest love.

And they have once again programmed this book with positive energy so that, by allowing the positive energy of the cosmos to enter them, everyone reading this book can, through this energy, heal and free themselves . . . Free themselves from burdensome elements that are no longer useful. Free themselves from everything that hinders the development of their consciousness and their connection with their own higher consciousness and higher intelligence. Free themselves from programs that were created artificially and never served the good of human beings and the human community.

Basically, these programs were burdensome stones on our path to the light and to our essence. Many such "stones" have already been removed, many have literally dissolved into light, because everything unnatural and artificially created is now returning to its origin. Everything is returning to its natural state.

Everything is returning to its true origin. The words of this book were chosen by the Pleiadian beings to enable us to regain our origin and our natural state. We will learn to communicate with light beings. We will learn to communicate with our inner being. We will find our natural intuition through the energy of this book. We will find joy in our souls and in our thoughts.

I wish you, dear readers, much fulfillment, countless discoveries, and endless happiness and love in your hearts.

With love and gratitude!
Your Pavlina

Loving Introduction
by the Pleiadian Orella

Dear Messengers of Light! We greet you from our luminous planes. We bring you valuable knowledge that can help you on your path to liberating your soul.

This knowledge will be about love, which, in a positive sense, is the strongest and most powerful feeling you can experience.

We ourselves also experience love. Love for our neighbors, love for ourselves, and love for everything animate and inanimate. Love, coming from the Divine Source, flows to each one of you and to each one of us. Love permeates every being and every object that may seem inanimate to you. For divine love is an existential quantity that gives life and divinity to all beings.

Love—the strongest and most powerful emotion known and felt by the human being—flows from an inexhaustible source. It flows from the source of divine love. This divine love that connects us all is an immensity that is completely independent of anything that happens in the outside world. But love is not just a feeling or a thought that you perceive. Love is the most powerful, highest frequency, incorporating absolutely everything. It incorporates light, colors, vibrations, geometric shapes, sounds, and other healing elements. It incorporates EVERYTHING.

Human development is returning to its essential core. It is returning to its natural state. Human beings are returning to what they have always been at heart—kind and loving creatures that honor others and themselves.

Human beings are now remembering what they carry within and what connects them with everything essential and with everything that has purpose in this life. And that is love—love in our heart, love for our fellow human beings. Our messages, with which we have accompanied you for so many years, are a continual guide and support, enabling you to discover the most valuable asset you can possibly find within yourself. All these messages—all these exercises—have been helping you to find the love within you, to feel this love and to pass it on.

I, Orella, feel a deep connection with you and with this topic. I love to pass on words of love because I know that love is able to heal every situation, every illness, and every burden that human beings carry with them.

The spiritual courses and teachings that you have attended and absorbed during your life so far have certainly covered a wide variety of themes. And yet all these courses and teachings were essentially aimed at finding the love within yourself and passing this love on.

This world needs love: unconditional love and unconditional, loving behavior and action. Without this action, there can be no unconditional healing of the diverse areas of this world.

This world needs love: every being needs love. And that is what our messages are about.

You may feel that the words of love in this book or in the individual messages heal your soul and your body, for each of the words we give you is programmed with the frequency of divine love.

You may experience how the last burdensome elements that need to leave your systems are transformed into light-filled frequencies with the help of the vibration of love.

You may realize that love is what you have been looking for all your life, unaware of the fact that the many different goals and tasks you set yourself in life had love as their goal. Perhaps you were all so busy with your goals, tasks, and life unfolding that you did not realize that love was the true goal hidden behind every theme.

You may not have realized that the outside world as well as the people and the beings around you, have repeatedly distracted you from your goals of love.

But your soul has not forgotten your true goal. It will lead you to the goal of love because your soul consists of light-filled love energy. That is its essence. It can therefore not miss the target of love.

Your soul may take a while to realize its goal—its path to love. But you can be sure that your soul will lead you to love and eventually set you free. It is impossible for you to miss your target, because your soul was created in the love of the Divine Source. In the light of divine freedom.

The Divine Source calls your soul to itself. The Divine Source sends out vibrations of love to every human soul, ensuring that it does not forget its origin.

Should it have forgotten, it is now being given the opportunity to remember once more.

We are all children of the Divine Source. Without exception. A source of infinite love, infinite light, and infinite energy. The high-vibrational light of love is the most powerful element in existence. And this high-vibrational light and this energy of love can be found in the messages and exercises in this book. It does not really matter what is being discussed or written about here. The high-vibrational light and the energy of love will permeate your soul as you read, enabling it to connect with its luminous, divine essence.

You are all returning to your natural state, your simplicity and playfulness. You are returning to your freedom. You move through this world, which is showering you with ever more light-filled vibrations, like young exuberant children. Like young children, you are once again joyful in the here and now, recognizing that you are connected in the here and now with everything essential, with everything loving and with everything luminous.

The words of love that flow to you in these messages and exercises heal your existence here on Earth and connect you with the existence of spaces and dimensions from which you have been separated—with the existence of parallel worlds, parallel dimensions, and parallel universes.

You yourselves are also parallel worlds, dimensions, and universes. You are parallel worlds, dimensions, and universes of your own being. In this time, and in this space. You had simply forgotten this important fact for so long because of the development of a society that wanted to push you in particular directions.

You yourselves are a parallel world and a parallel universe in one person.

Your three-dimensional perception has so far prevented you from perceiving parallel worlds, dimensions, and universes that are within your reality.

Your subtle perception has been abused and anesthetized. But the present time, which is the epitome of cosmic love, is guiding you toward remembering your abilities—and toward the full perception that is yours. The frequency of love helps you to achieve this. It helps you to reach the light of freedom.

The cosmic love flowing to you every day opens one door after another. And these doors, in turn, open opportunities for you to connect with divine love—this will enable you to illuminate your glorious being in this life.

You were created out of love. You have come from love. And you will all return to love. In this life. In the here and now. Not all of you have had an easy life. Perhaps it was more difficult than your body could bear. But your soul knew that, one day, the time of light and love would come—the time of freedom. Your soul knew that, in this incarnation within your body, it would succeed in absorbing divine love and divine light, and in healing your body through the light of love.

Everything is made of love. Everything.

And that is what this book, which is already transmitting the vibration of love to you, is all about—it is about the love in everything.

We look forward to this journey with you. We look forward to the vibration of love helping you with your all-encompassing healing. In love & devotion!

Your Orella

PART ONE

Liberating the Human Soul

1

The Separation of 5D Space from 3D Space

M any of you have already embarked on the path of love and have done a great deal of work in the process. Many of you have already traveled a long way and have never stopped. Up until now, you have had no time to pause for a moment and contemplate the beauties of this world.

You have had no time. The majority of you are still imprisoned in earthly time. Time, still relentless, does not allow you to rest, does not allow you to connect with your inner being. It does not allow you to connect with your higher consciousness.

Time, flexible and mobile, was previously a powerful weapon of the dark beings. The dark beings have taken advantage of their superiority and have locked you in a time matrix from which you can only escape with an expanded consciousness—your evolved consciousness facilitates your connection with all the spaces and dimensions you wish to connect with at this time. It connects you from a higher perspective with everything positive within this infinite universe. Over the next few years, time, which has enslaved you, will be restored to its original cosmic state—to a cosmic time state that is basically no longer time as you know it. As you ascend from the lower-vibrational levels, you will realize that time is working for you and not you for it.

You may have already realized, in this time and in the existing 3D space, that time is literally being torn apart and you are being given the opportunity to connect with another—extended—time. You have this perception because your consciousness has already, at least partially, connected with the realms of higher universal consciousness—that is how you have sensed that time is, as it were, standing still. At the same time, because the consciousness of humanity is increasing and expanding, time cracks are appearing in the 3D matrix, causing *time* to become unstable.

But not everyone has decided to leave the 3D matrix; many still need the experience of a low-vibrational life. Their free will is naturally respected. However, for those who have already gained experience and have opted for a world full of wonders, a light-filled plane has been prepared where they can breathe again and connect with the beauties of this world.

We would like to say a few words about that . . .

It has often been said that 3D and 5D will split apart. Many of you have been worried ever since, that when you leave the 3D matrix, you will lose loved ones and family members who are at a point in their development where they are still searching and temporarily lack knowledge. Many of you are worried that you will end up somewhere where you will be alone.

It is true that planet Earth will exist on the 3D and 5D levels. 3D and 5D will be separate spaces. However, 3D will be a mere illusion. It will exist for human souls who are still seeking their divine origin and who need this low-vibrational space to gain the experience they need. 3D and 5D will therefore continue to exist in parallel for some time to come.

For those human beings who have already decided to leave 3D, life in 5D will be very pleasant. People living in 5D will still be able to perceive the 3D world because, due to their developed consciousness, their ascension will also enable them to perceive different worlds. However, they will only perceive these different worlds if they so desire. Those living in 5D are able to move between worlds, dimensions, and spaces without even realizing it.

You are frequently moving between worlds already, without realizing it. I am sure you have often had the experience of only meeting pleasant people or finding yourself in an environment that feels loving and uplifting. In these moments, you are in 5D spaces and dimensions that have already been created by certain human beings. Your pure heart connects you with these worlds, like an imaginary bridge that connects you with 5D in a flash.

In moments when you have been at least partially in 5D, you have no longer felt any negative social pressure or time pressure. You have felt calmness, peace, and love in your soul and in your heart. You will find yourself in this state more and more often. You will simply feel more comfortable in 5D.

This will not happen abruptly. As mentioned, 3D and 5D will continue to exist in parallel for some time to come. The final division of these worlds will take place during the next few years. Depending on how much cosmic love human beings take into their hearts, this will happen at an earlier or later point in time. It depends on how quickly the human community progresses.

But right now, each one of you has the possibility of stepping out of your personal 3D reality. Each one of you has the possibility of building your own provisional 5D space around you. Your own personal 5D space connects you with the cosmic 5D space and, at the same time, it connects you with others who have accomplished their own entry into 5D.

Your planet has been preparing for her ascension for a long time. She knew that the separation of 3D and 5D was coming. She knew that 5D was her true reality for the time being, and that her journey would not end there. Her 3D form will be a mere illusion or hologram; a station for human souls who still wish to work through certain tasks for their personal development.

In developing, your planet wishes to join the cosmic, planetary community and, in this way, serve the higher cosmic laws. Your planet knew that, in her ascension into 5D, she could only take those human souls with her who follow and lovingly respect the higher planetary laws, only those human beings who were filled with loving vibrations and thoughts. Other human beings will not vibrationally match her elevated frequencies. That is the law of love and light, which must be respected.

Milin and his Pleiadian companions
Peace with you. Peace with us!

2

Displacement in Space and Time and Life's Possibilities in 5D

Leaving the 3D matrix will occur by way of an inconspicuous shift in space and time. You may not even realize that you are already in the 5D matrix. You will notice it if your personal state and the state of your environment is peaceful and loving. *Thanks to your pure heart, your transition to 5D will succeed. Or rather, thanks to your pure heart with the activated sacred chamber within it.*

We know that we have repeatedly mentioned the need for purity of heart. We know that we have repeatedly mentioned the need for purity in your thoughts and actions. But without this purity, entry into higher light-filled spaces cannot take place.

There is much more light and love in the higher realms of consciousness than in the spaces of the 3D matrix. All those with purity of heart and purity of thought can leave 3D. All those with good character, who wish only the best for other beings, all those who are connected at the same time with nature and its laws, will succeed. With love in your heart, it is possible to enter higher realms of consciousness; with heartfelt love for yourself and other beings.

Moreover, you can only leave 3D with an irradiated system of body matter. Higher vibrations of consciousness include love, gratitude, light, peace, positivity, and everything else that is high-vibrational and luminous. Everything that does not vibrate with light and is not loving or positive will therefore remain at a lower level. That is very logical and very simple.

Many human beings are eagerly looking into the most varied ways of entering higher realms of consciousness. Many human beings have still not understood that, for every individual, the prerequisite for this shift in space and time to take place is a pure heart and pure thoughts. This is the only prerequisite.

This shift in space and time is comparable with a shift in the time and space of those who have died. The dimension they are in is only a very small step away from your reality, in terms of space and time. You cannot see those who have died, and yet they are in your immediate vicinity. That is why they keep telling you that they are just a thought away. A single thought is enough to connect with them and their space.

Your relatives and ancestors who have died dwell in higher, light-filled vibrational levels. Due to their expanded conscious-ness, which connects them with countless spaces, times, and dimensions, they can see you whenever they like. But you cannot yet see them in your 3D reality. After your ascension into 5D, due to your evolved consciousness, you will have the opportunity to meet whenever you like with your family members and ancestors who have died. You will meet them in their subtle form.

Many of you have been waiting long for a meeting with your loved ones. Many have thought that such a meeting would only take place after your own physical death. In leaving 3D, you will have the opportunity during this earthly incarnation already, and rejoice in their subtle presence, their wisdom, and their evolved consciousness. However, only if you desire it.

⸺

We, the Pleiadian civilization, no longer experience physical death in the way you still do here on planet Earth. For you, physical death is often associated with deep grief and sometimes traumatic experiences that occur because of the loss of a loved one. For many people, the idea that someone has gone forever is very stressful.

In our civilization, a soul consciously passes into a new body. The soul also takes with it the consciousness it has acquired through its development.

Our community is divided into a physical and a subtle community. The subtle community—where the body has a subtle luminous or crystalline form—is a community with a higher level of development. There are very wise, luminous Pleiadian beings in this community with whom we often liaise and work.

Consequently, after a long period of consciousness development, and after leaving their physical body, many of our companions decide in favor of a light-filled, subtle form of existence. You could also say that these Pleiadians form the "Council of Elders."

For us, therefore, leaving the physical body does not mean the end of existence, as many human individuals believe it to be. For us, it merely means the transition to a different form of life.

The human community is also striving toward this development. Step by step. We wish you to experience moments of happiness in which you can continue to communicate with your departed family members when they are in a space that you human beings call the "heaven of human beings."

We wish you to experience moments of joy, when you meet up with your deceased family members again after many years.

You will be able to draw from their experiences, from their evolved consciousness, and from the kindled light of their soul that connects them with other light beings and other forms of life and being.

You may not yet be aware of what awaits you in 5D and of the possibilities that will open up to you there. Your senses and your perception will be developed through the increased light in your body. Sooner or later, you will become aware of your increasing ability to manifest and materialize.

True miracles await you, and we are delighted to be allowed to accompany you on your journey.

Milin and his Pleiadian companions
Peace with you. Peace with us!

3

The Healing Power of the Sun and a New Healing Symbol

In the near future, the sun and its light information will be accompanying you in a particularly loving and helpful manner. The sun has been bringing you life energy for a long time and, simultaneously, it is the mediator between you and the galactic worlds. It will now be sending you important information directly from the central sun of your galaxy and from the central sun of the Divine Source.

Your sun and its soul, Ra, are constantly trying to communicate with you. They are trying to tell you how you, as a human community, can best utilize free energy technologies effectively. Thanks to the sun's rays, human beings are rediscovering forgotten technologies very quickly.

Thanks to your sun, you are also able to receive positive thought patterns and positive emotions. That is why you feel so relaxed and secure when you are sunbathing, and that is also why you yourselves can produce positive thoughts and positive emotions.

Because of the cosmic influences and the increased cosmic energy coming to you, it is now becoming increasingly easy for the sun to have a positive effect on the system of your body. It sends its light into your system, light that is transformed into shades of color that your system uses for its own benefit. These frequencies can be perfectly absorbed by your chakras, helping them to heal themselves naturally. The sun also helps in the healing of the human body.

In this day and age, the sun is often taken for granted. But in earlier times human beings consciously worshiped it and its radiance. They healed themselves with the sun's light energy and communicated with it. And it was thanks to the sun that they always knew what planetary events were taking place. Each and every one of you came into contact with the sun-soul, Ra, before incarnating on this planet in this solar constellation. The sun-soul, Ra, communicated with you and told you how, with the help of the sun's rays, you could maintain your overall system at its optimum level of vitality during your earthly incarnation . . .

The soul of the sun told you that the best way to absorb the light energy of the sun for your spiritual and consciousness development was through the light chakras located above your head.

He told you that, with the help of your crown chakra, you are able to perfectly absorb solar radiation to support your physical body.

He told you that the time of dawn brings you vitality for your daily energy intake and the sunset a pleasant energy for your sleep.

By looking into the rising or setting sun, you also heal your soul. And all your chakras are given the opportunity to release faulty programs and to receive the positive elements of the light.

The soul of your sun, Ra, is a very wise being. He is in continual contact with the soul of your planet, Gaia, and with other light beings who are responsible for particular situations. Just like the earth-soul, Gaia, he welcomed you when you arrived on Earth and connected you with his natural matrix. In this incarnation you belong to the matrix of planet Earth and the matrix of your sun.

You belong to Earth's planetary system and to the solar constellation system.

On arrival on this Earth, you were fully connected with the natural matrix system and all its helpful aspects. But, over time, you began to slowly separate yourselves from the vital—and for you natural—matrix system, due to the manipulation of the human community by the dark forces, but also due to illness and other circumstances.

However, at this time, Ra and Gaia are increasingly making their presence felt and reconnecting you with their natural systems. Reconnecting with their natural systems will bring back your physical and spiritual power.

The matrix of Earth and the matrix of the sun have always been natural to human beings. Through persistent and extensive manipulation, you human beings have simply distanced yourselves from your natural state. It is almost as if you no longer belong to this planet, as if you have turned your back on it. Many people feel disconnected from the planet because of this manipulation.

People who are conscious of their spirituality, as well as those who are currently developing spiritually and in terms of consciousness, will be increasingly connected to the earth matrix and the sun matrix during this time. This will give them back their natural strength on all levels of their lives. Thanks to the crystal structures that the human body is currently creating within itself, the possibility of connecting with crystalline light information coming from the universe is increasing. And thanks to this light information, your DNA will be able to regenerate and fully develop. *Your light body process can begin.*

This time could be described as the time of renewal or renaissance of the human body, because the body matter is becoming more subtle. It is receiving subtle information from the Divine Source, enabling subtle systems such as clairvoyance, clairaudience, and clairsentience to develop more quickly.

Human beings wishing to develop on a subtle level can only walk the path to higher subtle dimensions of light in a subtle body. For this reason, the human body is currently undergoing an intensified cleansing process, enabling body matter to release any burdens that hinder subtleness. Nothing of a complicated and burdensome nature belongs in the natural and simple life of the higher realms of light. *Human beings are regaining their natural state.*

In your solar constellation and in the whole universe, everything is well arranged, natural, and of divine order. *And now the human body and its system are regaining their natural state and divine order.*

Little by little, you will come to feel that your own personal system is a well-arranged micro-universe that fits exactly into the macro-universe, with all its systems, with all its organs, and with all its matrix systems.

You will see that you belong to this planet and to its natural world. You will realize, more and more, that you cannot do without the energy of nature. You will understand that you cannot do without the sun's rays. You will become aware of how much power and naturalness you lacked when you did not feel absolutely connected with this galaxy. You will comprehend that this galaxy is your home.

We will now give you a symbol of the sun, programmed by us, which can help you on several levels of your healing, energetic cleansing, and regeneration process. We have connected this symbol, just like all the other symbols and number sequences we have given you, with the necessary morphogenetic fields.

Looking at this symbol will reconnect you with the natural matrix of the sun and the entire solar constellation. At the same time, you will be connected with information given to you by the sun-soul, Ra—information concerning how life happens on the worlds and stars around you, and information about other populated planets and their civilizations. The sun-soul, Ra, is the mediator between these civilizations in your solar constellation and your galaxy.

When you look at this symbol, you connect with the sun-soul, Ra, himself, with his wisdom and light-filled healing energy, and your light chakras expand above your head and receive light information from the sun. Your light chakras then receive their energy, their colors, and their vibration. This further increases the activity of your light chakras, and your mind is given the opportunity to travel to parallel worlds to which it previously had no access.

This symbol of the sun is programmed by us in such a way that, through the activation of your light chakras, your ability to receive information from the light world and its beings increases so that, through channeling, you can then make contact. This enables you to communicate with cosmic events.

How to work with this symbol . . .

Simply look at the symbol and you will be connected with the sun and with all the possibilities we have described in this message. Choose a period of time, intuitively, that seems appropriate to you. We recommend looking at this symbol for at least three minutes. In the following chapters we will tell you how you can use this symbol explicitly for channeling.

To reinforce the effect, you can speak this affirmation out loud . . .

Affirmation to Heal Your Mind

"I am completely connected with the sun and his soul, Ra.
The energy of the sun nourishes me.
 The energy of the sun heals me.
 The energy of the sun regenerates me.
 This connection with Ra brings me essential information.
I receive all these elements with gratitude and love.
 Thank you, thank you, thank you."

Milin and Wahou, together with
further Pleiadian companions
Peace with you. Peace with us!

4

Information Concerning the
Spiritual Purpose of Ascension
from Lower Levels

Now is the time to open up the realms and dimensions that will enable communication and allow you to discover new horizons. It is time to activate your subtle senses, enabling you to receive true and unadulterated information. You have had falsified and manipulated information for thousands of years. That time is now over.

The real time is dawning that will allow you to come out of your shell, stretch out your feelers, and look around to discover what really exists in the world around you. To look around and see what has been taken and hidden from you. To look around and discover what your senses could not perceive before, but now can.

It is time to find out that the world around you is so much more diverse and colorful than it previously appeared to be. It is time to realize that the world surrounding your planet is vast, and that other inhabited worlds and civilizations are your neighbors. It is time to understand that the world around your planet is made up of countless realms, dimensions, and parallel worlds that have been hidden from you for so long. Now the time has finally come to look around, activate your senses, and realize that much more exists than you could ever have imagined.

As always, we will proceed with you, step by step . . .

Let us start with the fact that you have been divested of your imagination. Your clairvoyance, which connected you with other worlds, was numbed so that your imagination lost its greatness, its colorfulness and its scope.

All that was left to you was three-dimensional perception. A perception that limits you in your natural, divine ability to expand your consciousness into surrounding worlds. You have been deprived of the ability to reach horizons that are linked to other horizons in other worlds and dimensions.

Through three-dimensional perception you were locked into the 3D matrix and its reality. That robbed you of your brain capacities, your DNA capacities, and any capacity for the growth of your consciousness. Three-dimensional perception has insufficient imagination because it is unable to connect with worlds of multidimensionality. It is unable to extend its senses into spaces and interstices of the worlds and dimensions around you. And they are in your immediate vicinity!

The manipulation of the human civilization, dear ones, was truly comprehensive . . .

But human beings have decided to step out of 3D reality. They have chosen to transform their dark reality into a light one, and they have chosen to expand their consciousness and develop.

With expanded consciousness, human beings will be able to step out of the lower-vibrational levels of dark realities and reconnect with worlds to which they had lost access. Through the expansion of their consciousness, human beings will regain the natural function of their sensory abilities of clairvoyance, clairaudience, and clairsentience. An expanded consciousness enables human beings to connect with other human beings as well as with other beings who have already developed their consciousness and are connected with the light realms of cosmic events.

It is necessary to understand that cosmic worlds, light dimensions, and other parallel worlds are in your immediate vicinity. They are not infinitely far away from you. They are very close to your reality. You are connected to these worlds via your heart, via the sacred chamber in your heart. And your light chakras above your head form a vehicle that enables you to travel to surrounding worlds and spaces. The chakras above your head are active and able to open doors to other worlds—provided your heart is pure. (You can find more on this in the book *Light Messages from the Pleiades*, chapter 4.) We will go into the sacred chamber of the heart in more detail in this book.

With your expanded consciousness and with the help of your higher self, you will be able to successfully enter the worlds and spaces of the cosmic world—through your higher consciousness and through the development of your spirituality.

The worlds, spaces, and dimensions that surround you could be said to be located side by side. You can enter these worlds at any time. Entering these worlds is dependent on your purity of heart and your determination. And as soon as you enter the 5D space, your heart space, you will realize how much you have been manipulated and influenced.

Your pure heart is the key to all spaces, dimensions, and worlds. Between these spaces, which vibrate at an extremely luminous, high level, there are essentially no physical boundaries. Everything is connected and interwoven. Borders only exist in the mind. Nevertheless, every space, every dimension, and every world is honored by the divine laws of respect and free will.

In contrast to high-vibrational, light-filled spaces, the low-vibrational levels are dimensionally closed spaces that are not connected with each other. Each of these low-vibrational worlds is practically self-contained and has its own individual frequency. It is very difficult to rise out of these low-vibrational worlds. Those wishing to free themselves from these worlds must develop a very strong will and great perseverance, because the low-vibrational frequencies of these worlds bind every thought that wishes to connect with the worlds of light. For this reason, countless light beings and peace-loving extraterrestrial civilizations are helping you—the human community. They understand this complex of problems. They understand that it is difficult to break out of the low vibration and that those constantly endeavoring to overcome the manipulation and step out of these low-vibrational levels often reach the end of their strength and endurance.

However, many of you have already managed to break free, or at least partially break free. Your subsequent connection with higher spaces and dimensions immediately reminded your soul of its light and its original divine vibration. And this has given your soul the power to connect with your light companions or with other light frequencies and to ascend higher and higher toward the light.

Anyone deciding to leave 3D or other low-vibrational levels is heard immediately by the light beings, and that person's wish is immediately conveyed to Divine Intelligence. Divine Intelligence then connects with their higher self—the higher consciousness of the person concerned—and begins to communicate with it and prepare a plan for a successful exit. This includes the removal of various karmic issues and any negativities that have hindered the leaving process so far.

During this time, when the process of leaving 3D is inevitable, a wide variety of issues manifest themselves—spiritual, mental, and physical issues that have prevented people from leaving 3D completely. Everything that has kept a person in the low-vibrational level needs to be processed or seen so that the person can move into spaces where such issues are transformed into light.

You could say that, right now, everything is happening all at once. But that is because humanity has been in a deep sleep for a very long time and is now undergoing a collective awakening. Everyone has an influence on everyone else, and the light of those who have awakened connects with others at the speed of cosmic light. The light multiplies and absorbs further luminous and positive elements.

Light attracts light, and many people who have remembered their luminous essence are already shining brightly and drawing light directly from the Divine Source.

Divine light is the highest-vibrating and most transformative light. And this divine light is just beginning to spread across the entire planet. However, there are many human beings who do not receive this divine light because they have chosen a different path for their personal development and transformation.

They have decided to stay in 3D for now and take their time in following their path.

For as long as 3D and 5D exist in parallel, those who choose 5D, who choose the transition to the fifth dimension, can find and contact these people at any time. You will be seen by these people, and you will also see them yourselves. However, their personal hardship will no longer affect you as much as it would have done in the past when you were still in 3D reality. You will see everything as if from a higher perspective.

The low-vibrational frequency of these people will no longer be able to reach you, because you have chosen a higher vibration.

And your light companions will only connect you with the soul light of people who bear love within them. Their negative elements will no longer reach you.

Many human beings who have decided to take this longer path of development run the risk of losing their physical sheath. But that is their own choice and their free will. Many of them have chosen to heal their souls in the spaces of the "heaven of human beings," where healing takes place through divine grace. This divine healing has been taking place since June 2021, healing human souls and human beings. It is a "healing and regeneration by the grace of God," as we communicated to you through the message of the same name in *Pleiadian Soul Healing*.

This wonderful time brings endless opportunities for healing and personal development. Everything depends on the decisions human beings make.

Every human being will retain their free will.

Milin and his Pleiadian companions
Peace with you. Peace with us!

5

Activation of the Pineal Gland with the Help of the Sun Symbol

The symbol of the sun that we have programmed for you also helps you to purify and activate your epiphysis—your pineal gland. By means of this symbol, subtle light information flows to you from the sun. This is able to dissolve manipulative programs that may still be in your pineal gland. These manipulative programs have created a dark energetic layer around your pineal gland and caused it to atrophy. With the help of this subtle light information from the sun, you can regain your natural state. *Every one of you is capable of communicating with the light world and its beings. Every one of you.*

Human beings are able to communicate via their clairvoyant senses. In earlier times, when human civilization was still completely natural and pure, every human being was able to communicate with every other human being by means of intuition and telepathy. People also used these abilities to exchange information with members of other planetary systems as well as light beings. The ability to channel was first developed by some human beings when their natural abilities in this respect were lost. This meant it was still possible for human beings who no longer possessed this ability to pass on messages and information from the light world to others. The pineal gland has always served as an antenna or amplifier for communication.

When people communicate with the help of channeling or mediumistic information transfer, we see that the pineal gland of the person concerned sends out energetic waves. These waves vibrate at different frequencies, depending on which beings or light worlds the person concerned is currently communicating with.

The more the person concerned devotes themselves to communicating with light beings, the greater the range and the expansiveness of the waves emanating from their pineal gland.

It is simply wonderful to watch people communicating with each other energetically, because of the very bright and colorful radiation of these waves. These waves connect both parties involved in the communication as well as the corresponding worlds of the beings involved. When a person is in light-filled communication, it looks as if their reality world and the world of the other being merge into one world. Then it is as if they are present in the light space of the being with whom they are currently communicating. There are no boundaries between these worlds. The only boundaries that exist are those that a person creates in their mind or in their imagination.

A person who communicates with light beings enters their world. Their heart connects with that world as their pineal gland receives information. When a person communicates with angelic beings, for example, they are present in the angelic realm, because at the moment of connection they literally merge with that sphere. This enables them to receive information from the angels. *This is only possible because all luminous worlds are connected with each other.* At all times, a perfect connection can be established with all of the light worlds and luminous dimensions simultaneously.

During communication, the human heart connects with the matrix signature of the divine world, while the human body connects with the light-filled signatures of the divine universal event in which all light beings are at home. If a person can manage a longer channeling session and establish a good, high-quality connection, then they connect with the divine world through all of their chakras. They find themselves in the beautiful divine signature, which basically connects them with the entire, infinite divine world and, simultaneously, with the world and the beings with whom they are currently communicating.

This signature is in constant light-filled motion and consists of circular formations. Everything is connected through circles, circular formations, and shapes. The information the human being receives from it is always rounded. It appears to them in the form of luminous rings, so to speak. Sometimes the human being is only able to receive a part of the information, only a part of this ring-shaped formation. But after a certain amount of time, during which they receive more and more information, they can say—ah, now it makes sense, now I understand the information, now I see it all. Now the circle is complete.

A person who frequently communicates with light beings, or other beings of good will, has very highly developed synapses in the brain. This ongoing processing of information enables the activity of their synapses and also enables the activity of their pineal gland.

Those capable of this kind of communication can confirm that their earthly life has also become brighter and lighter.

Through their communication with the light world, their personal reality is illuminated and their low-vibrational programs can enter the light more quickly, and be processed or neutralized accordingly. Every person who channels experiences feelings of happiness and unconditional love during this activity. This is because, when in communication, they are in a world of happiness and unconditional love—provided, of course, they are contacting beings from higher spheres of consciousness.

We would like to help you activate this innate ability to communicate with light beings through the vibration of our words and information.

In each of our books we have told you how important it is to take responsibility for yourself and to find answers within yourself. We have told you how important it is to rely on yourself and not look to others for information, to others who are unable to see inside you and unable to fully understand and advise you.

As the pineal gland is also connected to your higher consciousness—and your higher consciousness connects you to information from other light worlds and light beings—you will find that, by activating your pineal gland, your intuition will develop.

You will realize that your higher consciousness is able to connect to any world, dimension, time, or space.

You will realize that it is your higher consciousness that communicates with your environment and that not only your intuition but also your telepathy develops very quickly as a result of your expanded consciousness. This will make it much easier for you to find answers to all your questions within yourselves.

You will realize that your higher consciousness is completely connected with the sacred chamber of your heart and functions like a large communication unit through which the outer world communicates with your inner world.

You will realize that a divine power lies dormant within you that connects you with everything and with everyone.

You will find that the divine ray coming from your heart can expand into all the spaces and times of your being and into all the spaces and times of infinite, divine, universal existence.

You will realize that separation from the outside world has only taken place in your mind.

You will realize that your heart and your expanded consciousness connect you with everything. With absolutely everything. And your pineal gland will be able to send out signals and receive information that will bring you more answers—ones you may have been waiting for all your life.

You will realize that you are a part of this infinite, diverse, and loving event.

You will realize that the reality you are currently living in is a mere illusion that has served to expand your consciousness to what it was before.

You will receive more and more answers to your questions. And all you need to do is take time, every now and then, just for yourself, to open your heart, connect with Earth, and feel moments of the here and now. And in this moment—in the here and now—your soul, your mind, and your body merge into one. Your heart sends out a divine ray into the space of your existence that connects with your higher consciousness. And your pineal gland sends out signals and frequencies to worlds with which you intend to connect.

Basically, it is that simple. You can learn to live in the here and now. The present moment connects you with worlds you wish to enter as well as with information that wishes to reach you. You are able to receive. Here and now.

If you so wish, you can purify and activate your pineal gland with the help of the symbol we have programmed.

Use this symbol until you feel that light information is flowing to you perfectly.

But do not forget what else we have told you. Do not forget the present moment.

Exercise for Your Pineal Gland

Now contemplate the symbol of the sun for at least three minutes or for as long as you feel is comfortable.

Then say . . .

"Here and now, I make contact with my pineal gland. I send love and gratitude to my pineal gland.

I ask my pineal gland to receive the information that is currently reaching it.

Here and now, my pineal gland is purifying itself. Here and now, my pineal gland is being healed. Here and now, my pineal gland is being regenerated. Here and now, my pineal gland is being activated. My pineal gland is pure and clear.

My pineal gland is healed.

My pineal gland is regenerated. My pineal gland is activated. Thank you, thank you, thank you."

Orella, Ramuel, and Wahou, together
with further Pleiadian companions
Peace with you. Peace with us!

6

An Earth Symbol for Your Connection
with the Higher Order of This Planet

Another healing symbol that we have programmed and would
like to give you is a symbol of Earth and her soul, Gaia. As
we have already told you, Gaia also connected you with her information and her natural matrix system upon your arrival on Earth.

By working with this symbol you reconnect with the earth-soul,
Gaia, and all her frequencies. You connect with her natural matrix
system. You will fit into the system of this planet again like a key
into a lock. You will no longer feel as if you have lost your roots
and as if you do not belong to this Earth. You will again be one
with Gaia.

Even though your soul originally comes from other planetary
and galactic systems, you have chosen to live through your present
incarnation on planet Earth. That is why it is important for you to
feel a connection with Earth during your life here, a connection
with her beauty, her power, and her wisdom. We want to help you
root yourselves during your present incarnation so that you are
energetically nourished and protected.

We know that many of you have a deep desire to return to your
home planet. We know how strongly a part of your soul connects
you to your home planet and that you long for it. Realize that
you yourselves have chosen your incarnation on Earth. If you
manage to see everything from a higher perspective, you will be
able to experience your existence on this planet to the full. There
is nothing sadder than when a human being on this planet feels
lonely and misunderstood. Choose to live a life in which you
experience yourself to be full of energy and absolutely connected
with Earth and the planetary system you are in. You will then be

able to tackle the tasks you have set yourself more easily. You will be able to cope better with your normal life situations and your normal everyday life.

This symbol protects you with the power of Earth. It binds you to Earth and gives you the anchorage your body matter needs on this planet.

You should be connected with Earth every time you establish contact through channeling, because your connection with Earth ensures your successful connection with the light worlds.

Every time you establish contact through channeling, your body needs the assurance that it is grounded and that your soul and mind can expand as light and return to your body successfully after the contact has ended.

If your body does not feel grounded, you will not be able to establish full contact with the corresponding beings or worlds. Your body wants to feel that it is connected with Earth and that Earth is protecting it from influences that could occur through "impure" channeling.

In this way, your body protects itself from possible difficulties or attacks from entities that may want to harm it energetically. This is particularly important for those who have not been exploring how to connect with surrounding worlds for very long.

When you are well grounded, your body is able to fully experience these moments in the here and now and to generate a huge amount of light energy in your heart. With this light energy you can begin your light-filled contact, your channeling, with other beings.

Through this grounding, your body can send out a strong ray of light from your heart to the worlds or beings you wish to contact. And thanks to this grounded body, your pineal gland and your higher consciousness will be able to receive messages very well.

All this is made possible by this healing symbol.

This symbol also helps you to activate the light chakras under your feet more strongly. The activated light chakras under your feet receive Gaia's wisdom and information.

They connect you with the meridians and crystal structures of Earth.

The light chakras under your feet provide you with access to the luminous dimensions of Earth's interior as well as to the light beings who are located inside Earth and are responsible for these inner worlds.

They connect you with the crystalline beings who are responsible for your crystal realms.

You all know that crystals are your future. In your future, you will use crystals in almost all areas. Your body also consists of crystalline structures. Even your DNA and every single cell in your body contains tiny crystal particles. Every cell in your body wishes to activate its inner crystal sun, which it carries within itself and which has been smothered by the manipulations of the dark forces.

The crystal structure of your body, whose central place of development is the solar plexus, connects you with the crystal structures of Earth and with the crystal structures of your galaxy.

Everything is complex. Everything is complete and perfect. Everything fits together and consists of circles, and all is arranged with geometric precision. By working with this Earth symbol, you will be able to connect more quickly with all the systems of your planet. This is because we have programmed this symbol accordingly—just like all the other healing symbols and number sequences—and have connected it with morphogenetic fields.

Undoubtedly many of you who are often in nature heal naturally and connect naturally with the systems of Earth, the solar constellation, and the constellation of this galaxy. Spending time in nature belongs to your natural state.

This symbol of Earth is, in a way, an aid for connecting with the purest order and with the systems that Divine Intelligence has created.

At the same time, it binds you to new, luminous systems of higher levels of Earth that you are just entering, to divine systems without manipulation.

Systems that are heavenly and perfect.

It binds you to light information that is constantly streaming to your planet, helping you to successfully enter Earth's higher spaces.

We will move forward with you step by step. We want you to understand the complexity of your life and your being.

We want you to understand with every fiber of your being that your system fits exactly into the system of the universe. You are moving closer and closer to the system of the universe. You understand that your pure heart and a pure intention connect you with the purity of the universe.

Everything that makes you loving and luminous connects you with everything loving and luminous in this universe.

Your organs wish to fully connect with the systems of the planetary solar constellation and its frequency. Each one of your cells wishes to connect with the vibration of light energy that is all around you. All it takes is a change in your thoughts and actions.

And now the promised symbol . . .

It is enough to simply look at this symbol. This alone connects you with Gaia and all the possibilities we have just described. Choose a period of time, intuitively, that seems appropriate to you. We recommend that you look at this symbol for at least three minutes.

If you wish to ground or protect yourself before your channeling session or any other energetic work with the help of this symbol, you can speak the following affirmation out loud:

Affirmation

"I am fully connected with Earth and with her soul, Gaia.
The energy of Earth nourishes me.

The energy of Earth protects me.

This connection with Gaia brings me the information I need right now.

I receive all these elements with gratitude and love. Thank you, thank you, thank you."

---

*Ramuel, Milin, and Wahou, together
with further Pleiadian companions
Peace with you. Peace with us!*

7

Vilalata and Her Task
to Accompany You

Dear reader! I, Vilalata, will speak now and give you helpful information concerning communication with beings from the light worlds. Every one of you wishes to communicate and commune with beings of the light worlds and with the peace-loving beings of the cosmos.

Every one of you desires the opportunity to receive information that will help you in your further development, as well as information that will enable you to learn more about how the other inhabitants of the cosmic worlds are doing.

I know how much you desire this.

I know how much the dark forces and beings have influenced you in the past and separated you from your own potentials and abilities to communicate with the worlds of light and beings of good will.

I know and feel how frustrating your endeavors are when you simply do not receive the information for which you have been asking the light world for so long.

My Pleiadian companions and I are endeavoring to teach you, once more, how to connect with the surrounding world and with the beings that accompany you and wish to make contact with you.

I, Vilalata, have been chosen by my Pleiadian companions to open your channels to the higher dimensions of light and to prepare you to receive information through this form of communication—you call it channeling. I was chosen to do this and I feel it to be a great honor.

I know how big a task this will be for me, as I will be working energetically with each one of you individually. This is facilitated by the fact that you automatically connect to my energetic morphogenetic field and to my higher consciousness as you read these lines.

I can perceive each one of you, and I can feel each one of you. For many years, my father, who is a great healer, taught me the skills of communicating with the human community and healing human beings with the help of divine love.

I myself am very strongly connected with the angelic realms. Only loving beings exist in the angelic realms.

These realms are filled with love. Nothing else exists in them but love, light, gratitude, peace, and infinite understanding—the connection with all that is loving and divine. I can physically move in these realms of angelic beings and light creatures, and I am unspeakably glad that my father introduced me to these realms.

Every Pleiadian being has their own personal angel, as does every human being. Every Pleiadian being as well as every human being can connect with the angelic realm if they so wish and if it is necessary.

I have been given the task by my Pleiadian companions to be a kind of mediator between the Pleiadian community and the angelic beings and light creatures who are responsible for us.

I have been given the privilege of being able to enter the angelic realms at any time; and the love that comes from my heart opens the doors to these realms for me.

I was also required to pass tests relating to my person and to the purity of my heart and thoughts. It was not possible for me to enter the realm of the angelic worlds right from the very beginning of my training. I first had to prove, by means of countless tests, that my intentions were pure, as were my actions and thoughts.

The heart's love opens the doors to the realms of the angelic and light beings. Love alone enables a connection to be made with these beautiful beings.

Because of this, I receive information that I can pass on to those who need it.

My present task is to open for all of you the "doors" to the realms of the angelic beings and light creatures as well as the beings of good will who exist on the planets of this universe. You will go through a training program with me that will help you to successfully make contact with those beings and worlds with which you wish to communicate.

To this end, I will connect you with my heart power and my consciousness, which will allow you access to the worlds of love and light.

The light in your heart will become high-vibrational, enabling you to connect more easily with everything else that is high-vibrational and luminous.

For me, this is a great honor. I see and feel every one of you who wishes to make contact with me.

Thanks to years of loving training from the best teacher of my life—my father—my perception is comprehensive and fully capable of multidimensional projection.

I am able to work with each one of you because the power of my heart and my higher consciousness can penetrate all the dimensions, spaces, and times that need to be entered.

I am very much looking forward to working with you.

During our work together, the love of the light world will flow to you. It is my task to guide you to the source of light and the source of information, as you learn to act with increasing independence over time. It is my task to work through certain steps with you to perfect your channeling. But the ultimate goal of this task of mine is for you to eventually no longer need my help and for your work and actions to be your own responsibility. It will be my greatest pleasure to watch you become independent.

But for now, I am looking forward to this contact with you. As you work on connecting with the light worlds, you will feel my energy and my love. My energy and my love will accompany you and lift your personal energy and your personal light. They will accompany you during every moment of your work. Every word that finds its way to you brings you the vibration of my love as well as the vibration of the dimensions and worlds in which I am currently moving and in which I live. You will feel how beautiful life is in the higher spaces of consciousness, and you will feel what love feels like here with us, in the Pleiades star cluster.

You will be connected with dimensions of light and especially with those dimensions that bring you much-needed information. You will receive information that will help you to understand your reality and the reality of humankind from a higher perspective—from the perspective of the divine view of everything and from a perspective that makes sense for your own personal development.

You will understand that, until now, you have known very little about what this infinite event actually constitutes, this infinite divine event. You will understand, just as I did at some point, how complex this event is and that only when you understand it will the doors to the spaces and times of infinite existence open for you—for each of us.

Each one of us is infinite in our existence. Everything strives toward light and love. Light and love are infinite, divine parameters. Everything expands, everything broadens into an even greater light and an even greater love. Divinity knows no boundaries that could restrict light and love.

In deep devotion!
Vilalata

8

First Steps to Understanding Yourself When Channeling

We will begin with the phase of understanding, which will be worked through in the purest love. This phase has to do with understanding yourself, because the first thing you receive when channeling is information about yourself.

You will understand that you have actually long known the things you perceive or observe. The light worlds into which you are entering have never been foreign to you. On the contrary.

You will realize that the light worlds you gain access to, thanks to your pure heart and your expanded consciousness, are your true home.

Through the information you receive when channeling, you will learn to understand that everything is connected. Everyone is connected to everyone else. You will learn to understand that the light world knows no boundaries. It knows no boundaries in space, time, or thought. You will learn to understand that you influence the worlds you enter with your positive intention—and that you can influence them at any time. Because everything that takes place in these worlds is bonded in light, love, and gratitude. And that is precisely why you can influence situations or events in the infinite light world for your pure, positive well-being.

You will realize the greatness of the positive power of manifestation you bear within you. This great positive power of manifestation within you is able to change the entirety of the reality around you. You will find that changing the reality of your unresolved issues in your parallel dimension will have an immediate and positive effect on the reality of your earthly life on this planet.

Many of you have chosen to incarnate several times on this planet to take steps that will help you break out of manipulated reality. It is a story that has played out over many incarnations and which you now wish to conclude with a happy ending—through your entry into freedom, into a freedom that is naturally yours and is your birthright.

You will see that your hard work has paid off. Your intention, your work, and your efforts over many years will bear fruit.

Every light being responsible for planet Earth and for the development of human civilization is highly delighted with every step that human beings take toward their freedom. As soon as you ascend to higher dimensions, as we, the Pleiadian civilization, have succeeded in doing, you will be able to see and perceive those light beings that are accompanying you on your path.

You will see that light beings have accompanied you at almost every step of your way into freedom and happiness. You will be able to see how much support they have given you, how much work they have done to ensure that you recognize your path and do not miss your goal. *The light beings responsible for planet Earth have come to you directly from the Divine Source. The Divine Source is their home.*

These light beings, who have come to Earth to support you, have chosen to accompany you. This is a very challenging task because they are walking with the human community through a challenging time. These luminous beings have been tested by the Council of Light to see if they can truly withstand the strong onslaught of manipulation and evil that exists on Earth, for they are caring, peace-loving beings and anything of a low vibration robs them of power. *Therefore, the infinite love that flows from them to human beings is also being reinforced by the positive power of Divine Intelligence.* But all the light beings and angels who are on Earth and all the angels and light beings within Earth have chosen this great task voluntarily and are healing your world with their love. If they do need reinforcement, Divine Intelligence sends further angels and light beings who have also voluntarily decided to take on this task. *In each of the infinite number of spaces and dimensions in your reality, there are light beings and angels who are ready to aid and support you.*

All these light beings are able to perceive each other and instantly communicate with each other. The different dimensions, which you could say are located side by side, can merge from one moment to the next. At any moment, it is possible for several dimensions to merge into one and, in this way, make contact with any being at will, or gain an overview of the time or space in which your situation is currently taking place. Your light beings and angels are there for you at all times and in every situation. They also help you to step out of the not-so-positive dimensions and spaces and unfold into the light of freedom.

Reality is what people make it. When a person's thinking process is too complicated, they create countless dimensions and spaces around themselves, which are made up of all their diverse ideas and thoughts. A person who thinks in a simple and purposeful manner, on the other hand, creates a simple and clear reality that can instantly manifest in concrete form.

A person who thinks simply and clearly is not "overwhelmed" with dimensions that burden their actions and thoughts. Their real world is then also clearly and neatly organized, because they only manifest ideas that help them. By returning to your natural state, you return to the simplicity that will get you to your destination successfully. Your luminous helpers will also be able to accomplish their work more easily and gain clarity with regard to their task of accompanying you. They will be able to see more clearly which path they can help you on, and it will be easier for them to create situations for you that will strengthen you on that path.

The task of the light companions who are accompanying the human civilization at this time is very complicated, due to the fact that the dimensions and spaces prepared for humanity by Divine Intelligence are changing every second and millisecond. Every second, decisions are being made in the human community that have a significant impact on the destiny of humanity as a whole. At the moment, there is an infinite number of dimensions and spaces that every individual can enter and experience.

Divine Intelligence has not given you free will and free choice for nothing. It has created an infinite number of possibilities for you.

Possibilities that surround you at all times.

Your light guides endeavor, through your actions and thoughts, to move you toward the dimensions and spaces that are right for you, so that, in accordance with your personal needs, your further life path is as positive and simple as possible.

Your light beings are endeavoring every second and millisecond of your life to guide you in such a way that you make the right decisions, helping you to avoid going round in circles in the course of further future incarnations that would then cause you suffering and sadness and keep you trapped in 3D reality and its matrix.

This is the reason why I, Vilalata, am addressing you here. I would like to help you open the doors to the worlds of your light helpers and to learn to understand their information and calls to action. I would like you to learn to comprehend the words of love and understanding that they are continually sending to you.

Your light helpers have voluntarily, and out of their deepest love for you, decided to take on the role of your luminous companions. Through your expanded consciousness, your common field of love and light forms a bond between you, and you can walk purposefully, hand in hand, with your light helpers into the positive future that has already been prepared for you.

You can enter it in just one second or millisecond. It is enough to just think simply and positively. All possibilities have already been created for you. When you choose a simple, purposeful, positive path, these infinite numbers of dimensions and spaces merge into one whole, and a single broad path to happiness opens up to you, full of magic, love, and light. Your happiness cannot pass you by, because the positive decision you make will lead you to your happiness.

Your Vilalata
Peace with you. Peace with us!

9

Vilalata Talks About Self-Love
and Gives You an Exercise
with an Affirmation

Another topic I would very much like to address is your self-love. People who feel no love for themselves lose the ability to fully connect with the divine world of love. They are then simply incapable of communicating with infinite divine love and receive no feedback when they try to make contact with the world of love and light.

People who have no liking for themselves do not radiate the beautiful and almost glistening light that emanates from the hearts of those who bless themselves with the purest love and have learned to understand, respect, and accept themselves.

People who have no liking for themselves have a heart enclosed in a dark and almost gray energy sheath. The energy sheath binds their heart and prevents it from revealing its true power and beauty.

Very little light escapes from the hearts of these people. You could say that the hearts of these people look like half-burned-out fireplaces. A dark, gray energy emanates from them, which contains a great deal of sadness.

We feel great compassion for these people and know how painful the manipulation of their incarnations has been for them. We know how they were hurt, how they were wronged so many times that they lost their respect for themselves, lost their self-love and felt only pain and sadness in their hearts. Sadness is the cause of these people having no self-love for themselves anymore.

Sadness has been cultivated in them during countless incarnations here on Earth, and one could say that this sadness reaches deep into their "marrow."

This sadness leaves them unhappy and depressed, making them feel lonely and abandoned. Anger and fear that they cannot explain often arise in them, and they have no idea where it comes from.

However, it is not possible to find self-love again just like that. My Pleiadian ancestors' civilization also went through a long phase of sadness and fear. But their desire to ascend to higher levels as a whole—as an entire civilization—has given them ever-increasing strength to jump over their own shadow and shed their feelings of lack of self-love.

We know that it is possible to regain self-love, and we feel for those of you who are searching for self-love. I know that you will find it within you, and I see this development in many people.

I see that your hearts have been smothered and that there is not as much light flowing from them as there should be.

But I also see that many of you are striving to move closer to the loving and the light-filled once more.

A lack of self-love prevents communication with the world of light. A lack of self-love prevents communication with all beings of good will. Only radiant hearts resonate with loving frequencies and spaces.

I would like to help you to move closer to your love for yourself again, to move closer to everything that is loving and light-filled. I would like you to feel the resonance of light and love from those beings and human beings who carry self-love within them.

Every step toward self-love helps you to communicate more successfully with light beings and with your cosmic family.

To transform your sadness into joy and love for yourself, you can do the following exercise. This exercise is very simple. You will be using the healing properties of colors and the healing power of words.

If you wish to, you can connect with me during this exercise. I, Vilalata, will expand my field of consciousness and unite with you in this healing process.

During the exercise, you may feel that in some parts of your body negative energetic burdens that have settled in your cells are being released.

Together, we will focus on your heart, which will transmit the information to your entire system.

This gives the cells of your heart the opportunity to be reprogrammed to positive frequencies and receive the vibration of love.

I am with you, and I will accompany you.

Exercise for Reprogramming Your Heart to Joy

Imagine a virtual heart in front of your chest, in front of your physical heart, vibrant and rich-colored. The drawing shown here may serve as inspiration.

This virtual heart pulsates in a wonderfully radiant orange color. It is so clear that you can imagine it as a glowing orange-colored crystal. The color helps you to reprogram sadness to joy.

A beautiful purple-colored energy emanates from this orange heart. It is dynamic and animated. Purple is the color of transformation. It transforms the negative burden of your heart into light-filled energy.

Now imagine how this virtual heart approaches your physical heart. It comes closer and closer until it merges with your physical heart and bonds with it.

You can feel how this radiant orange transforms your sadness and any emotions in your heart that are not yours into joy and happiness.

This purple light transforms the burdens that previously bound the energy of your heart.

Now breathe deeply and say . . .

"My heart receives the light of joy and happiness. The energy of my heart vibrates in light-filled, divine energy.

The power of my heart unites with the positive and infinite power of love of the Divine Source.

I feel joy, happiness, and love. Love is my birthright.

The love of the Divine Source now unites me with my self-love. I love myself.

I love my body unreservedly, I love my soul, I love my mind. I love myself on all levels of my being.

I love myself.

I love my existence. I am love.

I am a child of divine love. I love myself."

Repeat this affirmation out loud three times in a row.

You can do this exercise together with the affirmation until you clearly feel the joy in your heart. You, yourself, will realize how often and for how long you should work on yourself. You can allow the heart that you have visualized to remain in your physical heart. You can let it unfold its helpful effect for as long as your intuition tells you to do so.

Every word of affirmation has been programmed by us.

Every word carries a strong healing vibration.

Your soul is able to decode the words and encode them into its system—these words carry the exact vibration that your system needs right then.

It may be that, when you look at the drawing or say the healing affirmation, you feel how the cells of your body release encoded emotions that previously prevented you from loving yourself. You might even get goose bumps or feel a chill run through you.

But even if you do not notice any reaction within you, that does not mean that nothing is being healed in your system. It is important to drink plenty of water after this exercise so that your cells and any stressed areas can clear. If you like, you can also transfer this affirmation to a piece of paper and program your water with it. Stick the piece of paper on the bottle or carafe of water, or place the carafe, bottle, or glass of water on the written affirmation for at least three minutes. Your water is then programmed and ready to help you love yourself. You can drink the water as often as you like—follow your intuition.

I, Vilalata, will accompany you in taking further steps towards successful contact with the light world. Finding your self-love, or working on finding it, enables you to make contact with light beings more easily.

Thank you for your love and for your trust.

With deep love!
Vilalata

Vilalata Accompanies You to Your First Channeled Communication with Light Beings

S elf-love simplifies everyday life. You will respect yourself and act in accordance with your kind-heartedness, making it easier for you to deal with other people. Your self-love will allow you to see life's events with greater clarity, enabling you to cope better with everyday situations.

You will realize that love and acting in accordance with love are the most important things in life. You will realize that this makes your life much better, simpler, and easier. You will realize that you no longer need to pretend to others because you will understand people like you for who you are deep down inside.

And if they don't identify with your views, with those in line with the love in your heart, that is not your problem but theirs.

Self-love will be your key to the worlds you wish to enter for communication with light beings and with beings of good will.

⸺

And now, I would like to take you through a channeling exercise for your first contact with a light being . . .

I will guide you and accompany you the whole time. I will take you by the hand, unite my higher consciousness with your higher consciousness, and open the path of communication for you. I will raise your personal light so that you can understand the information that is given to you.

I will be with you. You will feel me.

If you are communicating like this for the first time, be aware that practice is important. There is truth in saying practice makes perfect. It is necessary to practice communication and connection over and over again and not to give up immediately after the first few attempts. Remember that the reality of humankind has been severely manipulated in the past and that every human being must first find their way back to their natural state. They have to relearn how to use their senses, and they have to relearn how to perceive at a subtle level.

They must learn to be frequently and very naturally in the here and now.

The more often you communicate in this way, the more the number of synapses in your brain will increase, and the more your pineal gland will enlarge. The vibration of light in your system will increase. Your cells will become accustomed to higher dimensions of consciousness. They will long for this light and will not want to give it up. Your system will naturally lead you there to ensure that you do not cease your contact with the light world.

If you are someone who has channeled before, it is good to know that your communication and sensory perceptions are constantly evolving. You will not be limited in any way. Your contact with the light world will become clearer and clearer and more and more colorful in the course of your practice, and will expand to an infinite degree and scope.

I will guide all those who desire my help.

Channeling Exercise

Now, connect with Earth. You can do this by looking at the Earth symbol.

And while your gaze is focused on the symbol of Earth, say, "I am grounded. I am grounded. I am grounded." Imagine how all the chakras in your body shine.

Your root chakra shines, your sacral chakra shines, your solar plexus chakra shines, your heart chakra shines, your throat chakra shines, your two ear chakras shine, your third eye shines, and your crown chakra shines.

Ask your soul to unite with your heart. Here and now. Ask your mind to unite with your heart. Here and now. Perceive this unification in the here and now.

Let your heart shine and feel deep gratitude.

Now look at the sun symbol.

The sun symbol activates your pineal gland and opens the chakras above your head. This will give you access to the worlds and dimensions you wish to contact.

Close your eyes.

Now send a ray of light from your heart upwards to your upper light chakras. It unites with the light chakras above your head and rises higher and higher to unite with your higher consciousness.

Now send out your intention to the beings you wish to connect with.

Say the following words, "My purest intention connects me with my guardian angel [or: . . . with my light companion . . . with my cosmic family . . . with my family in the light].

I ask for information that is useful to me.

I ask for information that I can understand.

I receive all information with deep gratitude. Thank you, thank you, thank you."

Relax and let the information come to you. This can be in the form of images, words, colors, or shapes, every conceivable kind of impression and perception.

Take your time and observe what information comes to you.

Observe the form in which it comes to you.

If you feel you have received the information you need, thank them for it. Feel the gratitude deep in your heart.

And watch how your ray of light separates from your higher self.

Observe how it gradually becomes shorter and returns to your heart via your light chakras. Your heart continues to shine. It shines brightly and warmly.

And now say the words, "I [use your name here] have fully returned to the space and time of my personal reality.

My soul, my mind, and my energy are completely within my system. I am fully connected with Earth.

Thank you, thank you, thank you."

As soon as you have ended your contact, I, Vilalata, will also energetically separate myself from your personal energy. I will accompany you in your further channeling communications as often as you wish.

It is a great honor for me to accompany you. I wish you to be able to contact your light companions, your cosmic family, or your family in the heaven of human beings at any time. I am convinced that, in time, you will become so proficient that you will no longer need my help.

I hope you receive information that helps you to develop your consciousness and your spirituality. It can be helpful to write down the information you are given.

I wish you to realize that these light beings walk hand in hand with you and are never separate from you. Light beings are sent to all of us by Divine Intelligence so that we can feel the love and companionship of these subtle beings.

So that we feel that these light beings love us and are passing on their light to us,

So that they can remind us that we have all come from the Divine Source and have never been separated from it.

I wish you every success in your work. I will accompany you at all times for as long as you wish.

Your Vilalata
Peace with you. Peace with us!

11

Information on Contacting Beings from the Light World

Through intentional connection with the light world and its beings, your entire energetic system and therefore your entire organism will be illuminated.

Your cells will shine, overjoyed at your connection with higher levels, because your cells were created in the Divine Source of light, just like everything else in this infinite universe.

Allow us as a team, including Vilalata, Ramuel, and others of your Pleiadian companions, to now give you some further information concerning your future channeling of the light world and light beings. You will receive messages and knowledge directly from the Divine Source through your light companions or light beings. The presence of these beings alone will instantly connect you with the Divine Source and its information.

When you come into contact with these luminous beings, you will sometimes even find yourselves within the Divine Source.

And the systems of your body, soul, and mind will feel the divine frequency.

A part of your divine energy and a part of your divine home is brought to you through every connection with the light world. You will feel more and more that the light and purity of the soul are your true nature.

You will feel this beautiful divine energy within you and, after a while, you will also act in harmony with this energy, in purity and in love. Your connection with the light world will bring you an understanding of the complexity of what is happening in the light world and, at the same time, an understanding of what changes you should make in your everyday life.

You will understand that your actions may not always have been in accordance with the divine laws and the laws of justice. You will understand that you often thought you were someone other than you actually are. Maybe you underestimated yourselves, maybe you overestimated yourselves. You will understand that your guardian angels and light companions will always love you. They love you even if you feel that you are imperfect and full of faults. They love you despite your supposed imperfections.

Your guardian angels and your personal light companions love you unconditionally, under all circumstances and at all times. You will never hear words of "contradiction" or incomprehension from them. They will keep providing suggestions that offer different solutions for improving both your situation and your health.

They want nothing more than to see you joyful and in harmony.

And they will always deliver their solutions or instructions to you in the purest love. This is how you will be able to recognize that these come from the beings with whom you chose to be in contact, so that you need never worry that someone else might have attached themselves to you.

Your deceased relatives and your ancestors may communicate with you directly and straightforwardly. You may recognize them by certain characteristics they had in their earthly life. But don't expect them to always introduce themselves to you by name. Most of those who have died still remember their name from their last incarnation, but, for them, names from past incarnations no longer play a role.

In the world of light, those who have died have no need of a name because they recognize each other telepathically and through the vibration of their soul. Their vibration is their signature. If they communicate with you using their name from their last incarnation, they are only doing so to enable you to recognize them. After their physical death, names have no more meaning for them.

They feel their connection with the whole and their connection with the family in the light world to which they belong. When non-incarnated people communicate with you, you may notice that their way of speaking has changed. You may notice that their language is now much more refined and sophisticated. There is a very simple reason for this.

In many cases, they will have forgotten their personal earthly pain after their physical death because of having experienced healing. Healing through divine grace—which has had an increased effect on those who have died since June 2021—also heals their earthly pain. We reported on this in the previous book.

Every non-incarnated person will let you know in their messages that, after leaving the physical Earth world, they were given an understanding of divine existence in its entirety and granted a light-filled connection with it. Most of those who have died will tell you that "being" is much more than life in the earthly world, and that that was their most intense experience.

As you connect with *your cosmic family*, you will feel their boundless love for you and a deep gratitude—gratitude to be experiencing an incarnation in a human body and to be contributing to the overall liberation of humanity in this complicated matter. Your cosmic family will give you information and healing frequencies from your home planet so that you have the strength in your human body to master your task. This is how they support your incarnation.

You all come from different parts of this galaxy, many of you from even further afield. Distance does not matter to your cosmic family. Distance cannot separate you from it. Your cosmic family can energetically enter your reality at any time. It is only a question of whether you are mentally and physically ready for this contact and able to receive the information and high-vibrational frequencies of your home planet.

When you connect with us, *the Pleiadian Beings*, you will be able to recognize us beyond doubt by the healing Pleiadian frequencies and vibrations that come to you simultaneously with our arrival and the information we bring you. In addition, every contact with us will also bring healing to your entire system. But our light vibrates very quickly and so we can only fully connect with you if your system is purified, at least for the most part. Contact with us would otherwise be too intense for you, and your energy system would not be able to hold our energy.

In every contact with us, our Pleiadian light enters your cells, a light from the seventh dimension of consciousness. Whenever Pleiadian beings who no longer exist in a physical body but in a subtle one communicate with you, they illuminate your body with light energy from the ninth dimension of consciousness.

Understand that your cells, which until now have vibrated in 3D, must first become accustomed to the light of the higher dimensions of consciousness and release the lower-vibrational energy that they still carry.

However, every further contact with us will become easier, lighter, and brighter for you.

When you first come into contact with us, you may experience fatigue as your system releases negativity and then absorbs our Pleiadian light, which is simultaneously connected to the light and all the loving qualities of God.

But every contact with us will bring you healing, light, and love. Not just love, but divine love. At the same time, this will bring you the love and light of the Christ frequencies, as we are wholeheartedly connected to these frequencies. We will bring you the light of our higher dimensions, and in every contact with us your consciousness will feel the impulse to expand further.

This will also expand your knowledge and allow you to connect to certain morphogenetic fields that contribute to your personal spiritual development.

You will see that, through frequent contact with us, your personal light will grow. Your self-love will deepen and you will feel more love for other people. You will feel more love for all animals and plants. You will receive an overall view of your life and gain understanding for each of your actions, each of your feelings, and for your entire being. Your bond with people of good will deepen more and more.

You will receive a vast amount of cosmic energy that will connect you with the source of infinity, and your bodies will begin to regenerate and rejuvenate, thanks to the light-filled energies and the interplay of all the light information that will come to you at the moment of contact. Because your mind has understood the rules of the higher spheres of consciousness, your illnesses will leave you.

Even if the energy we bring for the release of your burdens may seem quite strong to you at first, our energy always carries our love, and this love accompanies you and heals your heart. We come to you without exception, and at all times, in love, peace, and understanding. Our information is comprehensive, but always helpful and caring.

Our intention is invariably pure and clear. We help you with your overall healing, with the development of your consciousness, and with understanding your general situation.

*Ramuel and Vilalata with
their Pleiadian companions
Peace with you. Peace with us!*

12

The Divine Ray Connects
You with Your Divine Plan

Your existence on this planet in a human body is precious and incredibly important.

Your existence here on Earth is for the greater good of humanity.

We know that your existence can seem trivial and insignificant from your point of view and from the point of view of three-dimensional perception.

But please believe that each one of you who has chosen to incarnate into this time and space carries within you a part of the divine plan that you were all made familiar with before your arrival on planet Earth.

You were informed of your task and of the actions you would carry out here on Earth.

Each one of you, enlightened and dedicated to the development of your light and consciousness, carries within you the divine ray that connects you at all times with the divine plan and informs you of the changes that planet Earth and humanity are going through.

Each one of you is a child of God, and each one of you is a messenger of God on this planet. Each one of you will be guided by the divine ray and reminded again and again of your divine origin.

Each one of you has a specific role to play in this time and space. You decided on this role in the realms of eternity. Every role is important and belongs in the mosaic of major events on this planet. Each role is a carefully thought-out plan of Divine Intelligence that will lead you to your overall perfection and the withdrawal from 3D reality that you so long for.

Events on this planet are changing at every moment. From our point of view, this looks like a moving whole that is constantly shifting and changing. Individual images and imprints fit together exactly, fall apart again and change, depending on the overall state of a person's actions and consciousness.

We see you as one big whole, even if this whole changes and moves every millisecond.

Every human being is surrounded by their own mobile, energetic reality. This connects them with others who are going through the same programs or who are still connected with them due to certain incidents from the past. And the reality of these human beings also combines in accordance with the extent and quality of their energetic vibration. They are connected with each other through time and space, and they are connected with each other through the time and space of their light-filled progression and their actions. Also, these people vibrate similarly, due to their resonance programs and frequencies. But they are connected by higher vibrations.

We see you as a whole, and yet we recognize each of you individually. We can perceive how the affairs of humankind are in constant motion and how each one of you influences the development and consciousness of the whole.

Everything is mobile. Everything is connected with everything else. You are connected to people and beings who live on other continents or on the other side of the globe. Your development, your actions, and your consciousness influence the lives of all living beings on this planet.

Every animal, every creature, every plant perceives your personal vibration and the vibration of humanity as a whole. Every element of this planet, including every—in your eyes—inanimate being, such as a mineral, is influenced by your personal actions and by the actions and development of society as a whole.

You truly walk hand in hand with this planet, with its cycles, with its kingdoms of nature, and with all of its creatures—animate and inanimate.

The light and consciousness of humanity is increasing as your time period brings great changes—changes that had to come. Everything that is happening on this planet is leading to an overall purification and illumination of this planet—one that has been in preparation for a long time and that corresponds to the divine plan. The light of humankind as a whole is increasing. You, who have chosen this light-filled, divine situation, illuminate the reality of this planet in accordance with the divine plan.

Through this, even if the reality of human beings seems clouded in some areas of this planet, the light of humanity as a whole intensifies and connects with the colorful structures and geometric forms of the cosmic world.

The light of your soul connects you with the lights of the universe. It connects you likewise with the lights of other loving civilizations that inhabit this galaxy with you. The light and the sound frequency of your soul connect you with the lights and sounds of the cosmic heights, from which everything essential is created—with the loving divine light and the sound frequencies of the divine world.

At present, your soul connects with these divine magnitudes and is guided by them. It is guided by its internal connection with the Divine Source. Your soul recognizes that which is essential at this time, which is loving, luminous, and high-vibrational. Your soul therefore gives up everything that restricts it and prevents it from connecting with its divine home. Your soul intuitively senses what serves its development and the development of society as a whole and acts accordingly.

In every moment of all that is happening on this planet, the colorful, energetic intensity of humanity increases and expands.

We are delighted to observe these happenings and developments.

We are delighted that humanity as a whole has awoken from this slumber that lasted for millennia.

We are delighted that the awakening of individual human beings has contributed to the awakening of other human beings

74

and thereby to the awakening of the whole. Even if the awakening seems slow from your perspective, we can say from our viewpoint that the awakening has taken place in record time and has started processes that are changing the future of humanity for the better.

The moving mosaic of events in each one of you and in the whole of humanity is heading toward a colorful and light-filled unity.

We thank you from the bottom of our hearts for your existence on this planet Earth.

Milin and his Pleiadian friends
Peace with you. Peace with us!

13

The Divine Source Is Located
Within Your Heart

You have been waiting for information that will "illuminate" for you what is happening in the light world and among its beings. Communication with the beings of the light world will bring you such knowledge. Through the reception of information, you will be connected with the vibration and the intimacy of your dimensions of consciousness. And these dimensions then connect you with your divine home.

Your divine home is your being, your essence, and everything that makes you pure human beings. Your connection with light beings brings joy to your heart, because you are connecting to a joy that is intrinsic to the Divine Source. Your divine home, from where you have come, is an infinite source of love and light. The Divine Source was not created in time, but in space. It has arisen in an intermediate space of the infinite event of the zero-point field, which has been there since the beginning of all existence.

There is no need for you to search for the point of origin of the Divine Source, because it has always been within you. There is no need for you to search for the Divine Source in time, because it has always been. Instead, you should search in space where the infinite existence of the Divine Source is to be found.

Time does not exist in the Divine Source.

Time exists on your planet and on planets where civilizations have been abused over time, as in your case. That is why you think in time periods and are governed by time. But in the universe and in the infinite Divine Source, time does not exist.

The Divine Source is an infinite happening guided by love, by the laws and rules of love. Love is frequency, vibration, light, gratitude, the infinite possibilities of colors, and the infinite possibilities of forms. Everything that arises in the Divine Source consists of infinite possibilities.

And love is what makes you divine.

Your soul, your mind, and the essence of your body originated in the Divine Source. The infinite intelligence of the Divine Source has given you form and properties—the form and properties of a human being.

And everything that originated in the Divine Source consists of divine geometry. You consist of divine geometry, nourished by divine light. All forms and all beings—animate and inanimate—consist of light-filled geometry.

You humans are so close to the Divine Source!

Your heart is the gateway to the Divine Source. The Divine Source is to be found within the sacred chamber of your heart, and the infinite happenings of the infinite universe are to be found within the sacred chamber of your heart simultaneously.

Your heart connects you with everything, with truly everything. You could say that each one of you is the center of the universe because the sacred chamber—your access to the Divine Source—is to be found within your heart.

The sacred heart chamber is physically present within your heart. It is an area, four millimeters in size, located on the posterior wall of the right atrium, where the deoxygenated blood from the veins flowing into the heart is enriched with oxygen and energy. This energy comes from the highly energized sacred chamber of your heart, which is surrounded by what is called the sinus node.

We have often mentioned this sacred heart chamber. It is through this that you reach the consciousness of the Divine Source. It is a physically very small chamber that leads you to the infinite qualities and possibilities of the Divine Source. This is because, in the sacred chamber of your heart, there is a zero-point field of free energy that connects you to the free energy of the infinite universe. It also provides access to your own knowledge and consciousness, and it connects you with the light world that fills you and surrounds you. When your positive, pure thoughts connect with this sacred heart space and the free energy it contains, it becomes possible for you to manifest your ideas and desires into reality.

The sacred chamber of your heart is activated above all through gratitude and the purity of your thoughts. Gratitude in your heart connects you with all that is light-filled and loving. It also connects you with light beings. Were you able to visually travel, by virtue of the sacred chamber, within your heart, you would find that this gateway—this portal—transports you to all the spaces and all the dimensions of the universe. You would realize that it connects you with all luminous beings and worlds in the universe. You would realize that you could connect with the Divine Source and its infinity in every moment of the here and now.

You would realize that the sacred chamber of your heart is the key to everything.

You imagine that the Divine Source is located "somewhere" in the infinite space of the universe. But that is not the case. This infinite space is within you. The Divine Source is within you. It is in your heart. You are connected with everything else through your heart. With all beingness. With all essentiality.

Via the sacred chamber of your heart, you can travel to all the spaces and times of your existence, regardless of whether you have already experienced them or are yet to experience them. This is because all time is one. Time does not exist in the light world.

We would like to teach you to increase your perception of your heart. Because your heart leads you into infinity. Your heart is a receiver of all cosmic frequencies, vibrations, colors, shapes, and information.

Please understand this: Your hearts connect you with each other. This connectivity exists in every human being. Every purified, light-filled, open human heart is a receiver of all divine information and especially for the highest form of life there is—for love. Every pure heart leads you through the sacred chamber directly to the Divine Source. Every human heart that has opened itself to the light is a recipient of divine love. *Your hearts, which are divine instruments, connect you with each other. And love is the key to activating these divine instruments of your body.*

Love is something everyone longs for; and everyone wishes to live in love. The higher the frequency of love that flows through the hearts of human beings, the stronger the connection between individuals and the stronger their connection with the Divine Source. This Divine Source of love is all around you and within you at the same time. You are messengers of divine love in a human body. You are messengers of divine light on this planet.

The purer your heart, the clearer your connection with your divine home. The purer your heart, the purer your connection with the light beings and your connection with the purest laws of the light world. One day you will look back and see that your efforts and actions were worthwhile. You will see that your pure heart has connected you more and more every day with your divine being and with all that is essential. You will see that you have made huge progress on all levels.

The sacred chamber of your heart opens up infinite possibilities for you, coming directly from the Divine Source. Through it, an infinite amount of light information and frequencies flows into your heart at every moment of your existence here on Earth. This is stored in your heart. It stores the light-filled frequencies and information from the Source and passes them on to your other systems, to the systems of your body, mind, and soul, and to the systems of your energy body.

This can perhaps best be compared to rays of light, a light-filled stream that constantly flows into the sacred chamber of your heart and then on into your heart organ. The sacred chamber of your heart, containing free energy, connects you with the Divine Source, which is also at home in the sacred chamber of your heart.

All things are connected and influence each other. Everything is one and connected by circular formations that provide a light-filled database of the universe.

Everything is one. Everything is connected. And this oneness, this wholeness, this whole happening, is able to expand infinitely.

In every millisecond of your perception, it is able to unfold in the here and now. In every moment of the here and now. Your oneness, which is at the same time a multiplicity of the whole, can be transformed in the here and now—transformed into infinity. Just as the Divine Source is in the sacred chamber of your heart, it is also to be found all around you, here and now.

In the moment of the here and now, for example during meditation, you feel your connection with everything. You also feel your connection with yourself. Time and space are one. You and the Divine Source are one. In the here and now, you are the center of the universe. In the here and now, the universe is within you.

And when you communicate with the light beings, you will realize and understand that what is happening around you is also happening within you.

You will understand that there is no need for you to look outside because you will find everything you are looking for within yourself.

You will understand that you are the center of the universe and that everything that happens takes place in your heart.

You will understand that your heart connects you with everything essential.

You will understand that your search is over as soon as you follow the rules and laws of love, because love allows you to merge with everything in existence that is loving and essential.

Your search will cease and you will be filled with the knowledge and wisdom that is around you and has always been within you.

Knowledge and wisdom are what make you divine, loving beings.

And now remember that we have charged every word with love, light, gratitude, and wisdom so that your hearts will be filled with the energy of this information. Your heart is able to receive these divine magnitudes and to heal by means of them. Your heart is the key to finding the divinity and wholeness you are striving for.

Orella, Ramuel, Wahou, and
their Pleiadian companions
Peace with you. Peace with us!

14

An Affirmation for Contacting Your Heart

Your heart is a divine tool. It originated in the Divine Source and carries the divine essence within. The cells of your heart also carry the divine essence that connects you to the Divine Source at all times.

Your heart cells have their own specific vibration. This vibration allows your heart to shine with crystalline light. This crystalline light creates its own crystalline network system within your heart that connects you with crystal frequencies from the Divine Source. Light information, which is then transmitted from your heart to your other systems, flows to you via this network. You could say that your heart is an autonomous instrument of your body, which is independent of its environment. It receives light information and transmits it to areas of your system that are in need.

Simply put—your heart is the key to everything and the key for everything. The electromagnetic light impulses that your heart constantly receives ensure that it is in perpetual motion, and its connection with the Divine Source is what enables it to work continuously. Through its connection with the Divine Source, it carries its own Divine Intelligence within itself. Every cell of your heart carries the Intelligence of the Divine Source.

Your heart is an expression of Divine Intelligence.

If you wish to connect or communicate with your heart, you can use an affirmation to do so. Your conscious decision and your realization that your heart is the key to a happy and harmonious life on this planet are of great importance.

It is important to feel gratitude for the fact that your heart is constantly working for you. It works to enable you to connect with the positive and loving frequencies of the universe and to connect with positive, loving people and beings.

The following affirmation expresses appreciation for your heart. These words of appreciation cause your divine heart power to radiate, and at the same time they activate the crystal systems that connect you with the outside world and with the light world.

Communicating with Light Beings through Your Heart Power

You can use this affirmation as a first step toward communicating with light beings. Visualize light in your heart and send a ray of light from your heart to your pineal gland. Observe how your pineal gland lights up. The brighter it shines, the easier it will be for you to connect with the light world and receive information.

Now say the following affirmation . . .

"In the here and now, I lovingly communicate with my heart.

In the here and now, I communicate with the intelligence of my heart.

In the here and now, I give gratitude to my heart and each one of my heart cells.

In the here and now, I bless my heart and every cell of my heart.

Through my intention, I activate my crystalline and light-filled heart power.

Through my intention, I activate my divine heart power.

Through my intention, I activate my ability to communicate with positive, loving light beings.

The luminous power of my gratitude strengthens my intention and opens all the divine spaces of my heart.

Thank you, thank you, thank you."

Orella, Ramuel, Wahou,
and their Pleiadian companions
Peace with you. Peace with us!

15

Orella Explains the Importance
of Every Human Incarnation

What else would I like to recommend to you that has not already been communicated by the group? Stay confident, stay in your psychic strength. Persevere and never lose sight of the goal you have been striving for for so long.

You are the ones who have come to Earth to help humanity and the overall situation of humanity, one that has never been experienced before. You are the ones who knew before arriving on this planet that new planetary constellations and an opening of light portals would take place, resulting in the dark beings and forces being rendered harmless.

You knew that the dark forces would do everything in their power to prevent the light-filled future of humanity and the light-filled constellation of Earth.

You knew that every one of you who descend to this planet would be playing your part in humanity's liberation and the liberation of all of you.

You knew that the divine ray you bring with you to this planet would combine with the divine rays of other human beings.

You knew that this time would provide a unique opportunity for you to free yourselves from your personal karmic issues and from the karmic issues of humanity as a whole that bind you to one another and weaken you.

You knew that your incarnation on this planet would not be easy, but you also knew that your path through this incarnation would become easier and more light-filled with each step. Many human souls have decided to incarnate during this time. Millions of them have descended to the most diverse areas of all the five continents of this planet, and have incarnated in places that are very luminous and high-vibrational. They have incarnated where they can transfer positive energy to their surroundings via the meridians of Earth and connect with locations you call places of power. In this way, the light energy emanating from these incarnated human souls is able to spread faster and more easily throughout the planet.

However, many other human souls have chosen a more difficult task for this incarnation and have incarnated in places that still carry a heavy energy. As human beings, they have decided to use their presence to illuminate certain areas and regions of the planet that still vibrate at a very low level with their divine ray of light. Many of these human beings can, then, only leave these places when the low-vibrational energy has been transformed and the beings there have been freed or have returned to the spaces and dimensions to which they actually belong.

Many more light-filled human souls have chosen to take on stressful situations or relationships during this momentous time and to incarnate in influential circles of society that are crucial to the development of humanity. After the positive "decoding" of the energies in which they are immersed, their light causes an energetic light explosion, as it were, which illuminates and awakens the relevant circles and situations.

Many human souls go through complicated situations or relationships that, without their inner light, would have brought a negative development to humanity in the future. The majority of these human souls have had a positive influence on those particular situations into which they incarnated, through the presence of their divine ray. They were often not concerned with processing their own karmic affairs. They took upon themselves the difficult task of helping humanity by solving issues in certain social circles. These are political, scientific, or social circles that have brought many negative things to humankind.

And every human soul that has taken on a higher, light-filled task has brought the light of the Divine Source and all its qualities with them to this planet.

Every human soul, every reader of these words, has liberated humanity through their presence. They have resolved karmic issues that have so far prevented humanity from moving out of 3D reality. Every one of you, in whatever form and wherever you are, has contributed to this bright plan.

You are all part of the overall plan. It depends on each and every one of you, on the intensity of your personal light that guides you through this incarnation. Never let the divine light you carry within you be smothered. Do not allow yourself to be led astray, and listen to your intuition at all times.

Allow your light companions and your higher self to guide you.

Your journey is far from over. Situations and concerns await you in which trust will be necessary. Trust in your plan and trust in the divine plan. Your trust will smooth your path and make the steps you take on your way easier. Your trust will connect you with people of good will who will help you on your way. And you will help them with your presence.

The bond between human beings constitutes a significant step, toward which the human community is striving. Your increasing connectedness gives you strength, stamina, and positive life energy for your path through your incarnation.

Always know that you are not alone. There are many of you who have decided to incarnate at this time to make your contribution. You may not yet know of each other. You may not yet have the courage to speak to each other. But the divine light that flows from your hearts will bring you together. It will connect you with each other and allow you to recognize who those people are who have come to this planet at this time with good intentions and a higher purpose.

Trust in and listen to your intuition. It will never fail you.

You will find treasures on your path that will open up the path to yourself and the path to communion with others. The need for communion will grow stronger and stronger within you, even though you will value the time you can spend with yourself, and the time you invest in your growth of consciousness.

But the feeling of connectedness and communion with human beings as well as with civilizations of good will on other planets in your galaxy will grow stronger and stronger within you. This bond will connect you more and more intensely and nourish you energetically. You will become a huge community, which will, in turn, be part of an even bigger community.

We are incredibly proud of you and we love you.

We love you with all our heart and feel a deep connection with you that fills our heart.

Together with you, we have embarked on an adventurous journey toward a positive future and the ascent to higher realms of consciousness.

You are already close to your goal.

We are with you, and we accompany you!

Orella and her Pleiadian companions
Peace with you. Peace with us!

16

The 21st Cosmic Key to the Liberation of the Human Soul—the Frequency of Cosmic Freedom

Step by step, the frequency of cosmic freedom liberates all those beings on this planet who have chosen liberation. Even in the dimension of eternity, where all beings exist in their luminous form and without a physical body, it fulfills this purpose.

The frequency of cosmic freedom is used to bring about liberation because of its intrinsic energetic quality and properties. Each cosmic frequency has its own quality and a variety of different properties, and yet all frequencies play together and cannot function without a common, light-filled connection. This frequency of cosmic freedom is also the most important key to liberating the soul of the human being. It constantly connects with other frequencies and brings human beings an ever-clearer understanding of their existence—of their light-filled existence, which originated in the Divine Source. The frequency of cosmic freedom liberates human beings and their souls through its energetic power. Only the liberation of their soul enables the human being to commune with the Divine Source and all its qualities.

We Pleiadians also commune with this infinitely powerful, all-encompassing frequency during our regular meditations. This connects us with everything that is luminous, peaceful, and loving.

We allow them to flow into our heart, thereby sensing our cosmic origin, our divine origin. We allow them to flow into the systems of our mind so that our thoughts become ever clearer, and we remain connected to the essence of our soul in the Divine Source.

We also need to purify our thoughts from time to time because we are often in contact with civilizations that need our help and vibrate at a lower level than we do.

Spending time in lower-vibrational levels certainly has an effect on us. But the unique frequency of cosmic freedom liberates all beings of good will.

Cosmic freedom is magnificent in its divinity. It connects us all and brings relief on all levels of existence. It brings with it beautiful rainbow colors—the whole energetic spectrum of free being—in which all aspects for a successful ascent into the light-filled spaces of consciousness are contained.

And this frequency of cosmic freedom has been coming to planet Earth for several years without you realizing it. It arrived together with the frequency of the cosmic love of Christ and has never left you.

We have told you many times that a new light, as well as frequencies of colors that you have not been able to perceive or pick up with your sense of sight up until now, will be visible on your planet. Recently, many of you have been able to see such color nuances in your sky with the naked eye.

More and more photos with beautiful color formations are appearing all over the world. In the near future, this color spectacle will become even greater and the frequency of cosmic freedom will be even more clearly visible. It will appear in all the colors of the rainbow or as part of a rainbow. This play of colors will appear in places on the planet where the frequency of cosmic freedom is particularly necessary. It will also appear in places where a large proportion of the low-vibrational elements have already been neutralized and transformed. That will make it easier for these colors to go to those places and appear there in all their glory.

You will be able to enjoy an increasing number of different color formations that will be clearly visible to the visual sense of human beings. With each passing day, the cosmic light and its frequencies, descending on planet Earth, will become clearer and more recognizable. The light of the planet will become more beautiful and radiant with each passing day.

Planet Earth continues to strive toward her goal of liberation, and she connects with all those human beings who walk with her on the path to light and freedom. You could say that, after a period of stagnation and imprisonment in restrictive frequencies, she has picked up tremendous speed and great momentum on her way to the light. And, of course, the population of this planet feels this.

Everything is happening at an increasing speed. In every second of human existence, old structures are disintegrating and systems are being formed. Everything is being molded anew. If we look at the human community and planet Earth from a higher perspective, we see the tremendous movement and reorganization of events and situations taking place in the system of each individual human being.

These changes and the introduction of new formations is also taking place in the family situation of each individual person—both physical and subtle—as well as in their social environment with their friends and in their immediate and more distant surroundings. People on this planet all influence each other, and their personal systems are influenced by the systems of others on the planet.

An overall process is taking place, a reshaping of the most diverse situations and structures. You could compare it to the coming and going in a beehive. Each bee has its own task, its own consciousness, its own activity. And yet the consciousness of each individual bee combines with the consciousness of the bees as a collective. And the whole collective of bees strives as one toward a common goal.

The human community is also striving toward a common goal. Every activity and the consciousness of each individual will combine with the consciousness of the collective and with the common activities of the collective.

This is not possible without the disintegration of systems that no longer function, and it is necessary for the emergence of new structures and formations. The frequency of cosmic freedom helps you on this path and gives you strength and endurance. This frequency carries the power of awakening and infinite freedom, boundless divine freedom—without envy, without jealousy, and without any other negative elements.

Invite this cosmic power into your heart, into your systems, into your whole, perhaps very challenging life.

It may be that your first steps in working with this wonderful frequency will be overwhelming, because they will show results faster than you would have expected. And these may be results that you had not expected, so that you first have to readjust in order to find your desired place in this magnificent life.

However, Divine Intelligence only gives you as much as you can bear. And if you trustingly commit yourself to your new life, you can be certain that the personal liberation of your mind, your soul, your body, and the most diverse systems of your being on this planet will succeed—especially as you are accompanied and supported by your light beings, enabling you to do everything through your own effort.

Trust and continue on your path toward light, love, peace, and freedom.

You will sense that this is the right path.

You will sense that this is the path to your own essence.

Greetings from Orin
Peace with you. Peace with us!

17

Release from Stressful Energetic Programs
Caused by Written or Verbal Contracts

Although this time is already very light-filled in terms of frequency and the cosmic light is increasingly reaching the surface as well as the interior of this planet, dark energies are still at work here, now and then attempting to hijack human beings or divert them from the path they have chosen for this incarnation.

Although these dark entities no longer have the same power as before, it is helpful to maintain a good physical and psychological condition by purifying yourself with light from time to time and protecting yourself from foreign, low-vibrational energies.

Over time, we have given you several ways to protect yourselves energetically, such as the exercise in *Pleiadian Soul Healing* for protecting your aura and your system through the power of your words. In that book, we also introduced you for the first time to the "Light Fountain" exercise for purifying all human systems.

Of course, your decision not to allow negative energies into your system is always the most important protection. But what should you do if, despite your decision, foreign, low-vibrational energies approach you and make life difficult?

Maybe you have already taken steps in this regard. Maybe you have already implemented energetic measures and yet you are still unable to raise your personal energy, meaning that your life is not moving in the direction you would like it to.

There could be a specific reason for this.

There may be energetic programs in your system that become activated the moment certain people, beings, or energies are near you. It may be that these people, beings, or energies remind you of burdens from past times. They may activate the energetic programs of old "contracts" in you. Time and again, people have taken steps toward the light and toward healing themselves. They have tried all sorts of things, only to find that, when they come into contact with light energy or the purest cosmic energies, they feel bad and everything within them that is light-filled collapses, even though they yearn for contact with light energy so much.

Perhaps you are one of these people, and perhaps the reason for this is that you once found yourself in a situation in which you never wanted to be.

Perhaps in a past life—or in this one—you have felt that someone has manipulated you into a situation or kept you in an energy that you could not bear. You may have allowed yourself to be persuaded to adopt a particular viewpoint or to act in ways that you would never have done under normal circumstances. This might mean that you now have programs caused by contracts from past times that coerce you into acting or behaving in a certain way. You may not recognize this as coercion, but instead consider it to be completely rational thinking and behavior.

Dark beings and powers have very often used this "technique," not only in your present time but also since the beginning. They have sown such programs in people's systems before now. Such programs can easily be activated to prevent people from escaping dependency in their current incarnations.

This happened again at the beginning of 2020. At the beginning of that year, energetic programs and contracts from past times were opened and activated, manipulating the thinking and behavior of countless millions of people without them realizing it.

Their light beings reminded these people of the light of their path and the light of their soul, but not all of them remained conscious of their divine essence and were able to continue or resume their original path.

Not all human beings were granted this. Not all could be sufficiently reminded of their light nature. Many still need help and support to gradually realize why this mass manipulation and countless other negative situations have come about.

Always remember: Many of you already know that it served to hinder your unique destiny, because people who are light-filled in their souls come to this planet with a light-filled task. Your task is to awaken to freedom. The dark beings know of this task. That is why they have largely forced light-filled human beings to sign contracts, or confirm them verbally, even before their current incarnation, keeping them in captivity to this day.

The negative forces prevent human beings from gaining their freedom. They want to make human beings forget that freedom is their greatest desire in life.

If you are one of those who feel they need to dissolve contracts, make that decision NOW. Your decision will help you to free yourself from the captivity of contracts, no matter what kind of contracts they might be.

If you want to dissolve such contracts, it is necessary to become aware that they are low-vibrational programs that activate when they come into contact with low-vibrational energies. But even when they come into contact with light energy, these programs begin having a low-vibrational effect on the person concerned.

The person's strength is depleted more and more, and their overall condition is increasingly weakened.

These programs carry their own intelligence, which is connected to the intelligence of low-vibrational beings and powers. This intelligence "sleeps" and remains quiet in a person as long as it feels no threat from the light and its vibration. However, should they feel threatened, then at some point the energy of these programs will influence your systems.

Not always, but in many cases, these contract programs have been coded into a wide variety of spaces, dimensions, and times, ensuring that people cannot free themselves from them so easily. If such contracts are then activated, the duplicates or copies of the contracts on these levels are also activated.

Such contracts can also be activated in those parts of a person's soul that did not incarnate with them in this space and time. Every human soul is multidimensional and some parts of this soul are present in other people on this planet, on other planets, in the heaven of human beings, or in various parallel worlds. All soul parts belonging to a soul family can therefore be influenced.

But realize that you can change it!

In the here and now, it is possible for you to connect with all your soul parts and simultaneously with all the spaces, dimensions, times, and parallel worlds in which your soul parts are present, waiting to be released.

In the here and now, you are capable of complete connection with all the components of your present self and of connection with your higher self—thanks to your higher consciousness and thanks to all the elements of the divine world of light and its beings.

The here and now can bring you holistic healing. It can bring you liberation and complete freedom. The present moment and your connection with your heart are the key to healing your system.

And not only can you free yourself from contract programs in the here and now, you can also lead your human soul toward its highest evolution: absolute spiritual freedom. This total liberation—this path to absolute freedom—enables you to connect with the spaces of cosmic freedom and infinity.

Your path to absolute freedom, to total liberation, allows you to enter the system of those beings who have already attained their personal freedom and their holistic connection with the purest cosmic spaces. All liberated and free beings are in the system of the purest cosmic level and belong to the system of the 21st cosmic frequency, which helps beings who are on the path of liberation.

You already know this frequency as the 21st key to the transition to the Golden Age.

In the book *Light Messages from the Pleiades* you will also find an Affirmation for Attaining Cosmic Freedom.

Light beings who are connected with the 21st cosmic frequency work with this frequency. Ascended Masters who have achieved their personal freedom during their incarnation on planet Earth, and have therefore been accepted into the system of the 21st frequency of cosmic freedom, work with it.

We would now like to help you to remove from your systems the energetic programs of those contracts that are hindering your personal, complete liberation.

We offer you an exercise that contains an affirmation. Each word of this affirmation is positively, energetically charged by us. Speaking this affirmation can help you to dissolve burdensome contract programming in your overall system and neutralize it in the divine light of freedom.

In this exercise, you will work with the number sequence 3717, which we call the "number sequence of trust."

It enables you to energetically enter our Pleiadian star and connects you with the consciousness level of us Pleiadians. It is charged with our personal protection and enables you to grow spiritually.

Exercise to Free Yourself from Burdensome Energy Contracts

Breathe deeply several times and say, "**3717. 3717. 3717.**"

Then call all your light beings to you and tell them of your intention to free yourself from all burdensome multidimensional energetic contracts. Focus your attention on your heart and let it shine radiantly. Now activate the frequency of gratitude in your heart. Imagine that the word "gratitude" is floating in front of your heart. You can see how each letter vibrates with light. Now watch as the individual letters dissolve into luminous, radiant energy and form a cloud of light in front of your heart.

This light energy then flows into the sacred chamber of your heart. As soon as the light energy flows into your sacred heart chamber, you connect with the light beings of cosmic freedom. Your intention is sufficient.

Ask them for support in this energetic process. Ask them to connect your system to the 21st cosmic key for the transition to cosmic freedom. This enables you to merge with divine energy, wholeness, and freedom.

Through this frequency you can move toward neutralizing the energetic programs of burdensome contracts. The light beings will help you.

Now take another deep breath and say . . .

"Here and now. Now, and in this space, I make the conscious decision to dissolve and neutralize all negative programs of written and verbal contracts, in all spaces, times, dimensions, intermediate dimensions, and parallel worlds of my overall existence.

Now, and in this space, I make the conscious decision to dissolve and neutralize all negative programs of written and verbal contracts, in all parts of my soul that belong to me in all spaces, times, dimensions, intermediate dimensions, and parallel worlds of my overall existence.

In the here and now, the 21st frequency of cosmic freedom dissolves and neutralizes absolutely all negative programs of all written and verbal contracts in all times, spaces, dimensions, intermediate dimensions, and parallel worlds of my total existence and in all parts of my soul that are mine.

The light beings of cosmic freedom bring absolute freedom into the system of my soul, my mind, my body, and into all systems of all soul parts that are mine. All burdensome programs of written and verbal contracts are canceled, neutralized, and transformed into the light of cosmic freedom.

I forgive all those people and beings who have bound me through the programs of written and verbal contracts.

My forgiveness is absolute. My forgiveness sets us all free.

I confirm, now and in this space, the liberation of all the systems of my soul, all the systems of my mind, and all the systems of my body.

Thank you, thank you, thank you."

Repeat this affirmation two more times, then consciously thank all the light beings who have worked with you. Finally, ensure that the new energy conditions are protected. To do this, scan your body with the help of the light fountain.

This exercise goes as follows . . .

Fixing the New Energy State
Through the "Light Fountain"

Imagine that golden light from the cosmos reaches your crown chakra.

This golden light enters your crown chakra and flows down into your heart.

Now imagine that the purest light and the energy of Earth are rising through the soles of your feet and flowing to your heart. Imagine this energy too as golden in color.

The light energy of the cosmos and the Earth meet in your heart. Their current is so strong that you can watch a fountain of light emerge from your heart. The rays of this light flow in all directions and into all the spaces of your body and aura. They flow into all the spaces of your existence.

You can let the light of these rays spread out as far as you like. Visualize this light for as long as your intuition tells you to.

Now ask the beings of cosmic freedom to integrate and activate the 21st frequency of cosmic freedom in the systems of your soul, mind, and body.

You should do this exercise at least three times at intervals that seem appropriate to you. If necessary, do it as often as you need to until you feel an improvement and can effortlessly raise your energy during your light work.

---

*I wish you infinite freedom
for your life and your being!*

Ramuel

18

Your First Name Brings You Vitality and Cosmic Energy

In this important time, human beings are turning more and more to their essence and origin. The development of humankind is proceeding in a spiral. The spiral form connects the human community with the sacred geometry of the universe, with all the circular forms held by the universe in the database of its consciousness, programmed by Divine Intelligence.

Every molecule, every atom, every neutron, every proton, and every other smallest particle in the universe is connected to Divine Intelligence. Divine Intelligence is in absolutely everything. There is also a part of Divine Intelligence and its energy in every human being.

Each one of you is connected with this infinite greatness. Each of you carries an enormous number of elements of Divine Intelligence within you to guide you through this incarnation.

One special divine element that you carry is your first name. You have chosen your first name for the duration of this current incarnation, and Divine Intelligence has programmed your first name with its divine, sustaining power.

Even if you did not like your name as a child or could not identify with it, be sure that you chose your first name yourself. You whispered it to your parents, in their thoughts, before you physically entered this world.

In all likelihood, you chose this name, after consulting with your parents or family members, when you were still in the dimensions of the heaven of human beings.

Everything has its meaning. Every word has its meaning. And the vibration of every word also has its meaning. Your first name was programmed for your life energy, your power, and your protection by Divine Intelligence.

You may have had a different name in your last incarnation, or you may have had this name for many incarnations. You may decide on a different name in your next incarnation, or you may keep it . . .

That depends on you and your intentions for your next incarnation.

Everything has a purpose and nothing happens by chance. It is also no coincidence that you are just now becoming aware of what we are about to tell you. It has to do with the intention you had when you chose your first name, before coming to this Earth.

You may have forgotten the great significance your first name has for you, what great power and energy it carries. The divine power and energy of your first name has accompanied you your whole life. It will now accompany you with even more strength and purpose if you remember this fact, keep it in your awareness, and use the many positive qualities of your name from now on.

In the realms of the Divine Source there is an imprint of the energy of your first name enabling you to connect with the energy of this imprint at any time.

Your first name carries a tone, a vibration, a color, and a certain geometric shape that connects you with the sacred geometry of the universe.

Your name can therefore also promote your healing and your connection with your original body energy.

Your first name is responsible for you in this incarnation and brings you the accompanying power of the Divine Source. Therefore, sing your first name. Say it out loud. Paint it and decorate it in the most beautiful colors that intuitively come to mind. Visualize your name. Bless your name. Program your first name into high-quality water and send it the gratitude of your heart.

Act intuitively. You will feel the great power your name unfolds for you. It will provide you with the energy you have chosen and which, through carelessness and unconsciousness, has somehow been pushed into a corner and forgotten. It will bring it out into the open again.

A Useful Exercise for Your First Name

If you have several first names, please use your own judgement and intuitively choose the name or names you feel are positively associated with you. In the past, children were often given additional first names because of family tradition.

Act and decide from the power of your heart.

And if you like, write your first name on a piece of paper. You can use whatever colors you like. Choose them intuitively as well.

Bless every letter of your name. Bless your whole name.

Now look at your blessed name on the paper for the period of time that seems appropriate to you.

Send the gratitude of your heart to your name.

And now say . . .

"In the here and now, I bind myself to the energy, power, and intelligence of my first name.

My first name gives me infinite vitality, divine energy, and protection.

My first name connects me absolutely and comprehensively with the Divine Source.

My first name is [pronounce it three times in a row]."

Now look at your first name written on the piece of paper. The colors you have intuitively chosen are most likely the colors of its energetic imprint in the Divine Source. These colors strengthen you and bring you life energy for your system and for your path through your earthly incarnation.

Ramuel and his Pleiadian companions
Peace with you. Peace with us!

19

The Atlanteans and the Civilizations in Earth's Interior Prepare for Contact and the Transfer of Technologies

Have trust in this time period. Trust that you are on the right path. You are not alone on this path. A large number of human souls have descended to this planet to help with the overall ascent. And not only human souls, but also the souls of cosmic populations.

It is moving to observe how many extraterrestrial, peace-loving civilizations are taking part in this colossal ascension. *It is moving to observe* how many souls, sent to this planet, are assisting the human community.

It is moving to observe how many of those sent are connecting in a light-filled and loving way to help human beings and planet Earth to shine again in their full and original beauty.

Peace-loving civilizations, in their physical form within planet Earth, are also beginning to connect with the human civilization on Earth's surface. Civilizations that decided to live in Earth's interior after the destruction of Atlantis are now also beginning to speak out more frequently—still mainly in a subtle way—and provide information about their existence. Physical civilizations that were on this planet in times long past have never completely ceased to exist. When Atlantis was destroyed, many retreated into Earth's interior and built a new form of life there. Since then, many of them have visited Earth's surface from time to time—not only in subtle form—and sometimes appear in the space dimensions in which humanity exists at the moment. But soon, conscious connection with the human community and regular visits to Earth's surface will be possible.

Many of those human beings whose consciousness is highly developed know of the existence of these ancient civilizations. They suspect that the human community on this planet is in for a big surprise—and they are looking forward to it!

Earth began to regenerate very quickly once the malevolent extraterrestrial civilizations and beings had left Earth's interior. The cosmic conditions and the increased influx of cosmic light are benefiting this process. Since then, light beings and angels in the spaces and dimensions of Earth's interior have also been constantly increasing their light and light vibration and sending healing frequencies to the human community. They connect with the light beings and angels of human beings and, in this way, help them to rediscover their natural, original energy.

Now, the physical and subtle civilizations of Earth's interior are also looking forward to finally being able to officially bring their energy and information to the surface of planet Earth and hand it over to her human inhabitants.

For a very long time, the existence of these innerterrestrials was kept secret, because the human community was unable to accept the existence of such civilizations. And another reason why encounters with human beings have been rare so far is their light-filled physical vibration. Their vibration is so high that the lower-vibrational matter of today's human beings would not have been able to withstand the contact. That is another reason why a meeting has been practically impossible.

Members of those civilizations who decided to live in Earth's interior after the fall of their land are very highly developed beings whose consciousness far exceeds that of the consciousness of human beings. Their consciousness is still connected with the collective consciousness of their existence as a whole. They are in constant contact with areas of their civilization that are located in other dimensions or spaces, or on other planets. Their knowledge of technology is so high that it would take the human civilization several hundred thousand years to reach a similar stage if it were to develop normally.

Their high-level technology is linked to the purest laws of divine order and Divine Intelligence. Their lifestyle is such that they do not abuse the energetic and material resources of planet Earth.

Instead, they utilize the divine free energy that is available practically everywhere.

While subterranean civilizations have rarely sought contact with human beings on the surface, peace-loving extraterrestrial civilizations have been supporting human beings for a long time. They have developed a wide variety of technologies with which to help the human organism, and have been waiting for the right time to officially hand over their knowledge to the human community.

Many of their technologies, which are to be passed on to humanity, also function on the basis of free energy and utilize cosmic divine light and its intelligence as a source of energy. They are light-filled, high-vibrational technologies that can return the human organism and various systems of the human community to their original order.

Human beings should really be very happy. With the help of these technologies, those of you who are consciously prepared to heal and regenerate will be able to harmonize your body, your home, and various areas of your life in a natural way, in a very short time. Technologies based on free energy will replace the energy sources that humankind has used until now and still considers to be irreplaceable, such as electricity, oil, gas, and coal. A whole range of technologies is already at hand for the human community that will help it return to its original, natural, and divine state. We are still waiting for certain exchanges to take place on the political and economic level. This has so far prevented the pure reception and utilization of these technologies. We are still waiting for the expansion of the consciousness of human beings, which will enable them to accept these technologies with the purest of intentions.

Technologies for the regeneration and development of the human body have been prepared that utilize the purest cosmic energy of the cosmos, technologies that make use of the surrounding planets with which human beings will connect energetically. Human beings will connect with the energy, vibration, and other elements of the surrounding planets of this solar system in accordance with their natural order.

Technologies that will help the human body, mind, and soul to heal, to regenerate, and to develop consciousness utilize the frequencies and light information of the sun. Capsules will be prepared for internal ingestion, which contain the light-filled, living energy of the sun. They will illuminate human beings from the inside, bringing solar energy into their systems and serving to increase their DNA function, all thanks to their light information. These capsules have their own consciousness, and their intelligence is connected directly and without spatial or temporal separation with the sun, its soul, Ra, and with all the information that the sun carries within itself. Such natural technologies will heal human beings. The frequencies and properties of colors will also be used, because every color carries cosmic elements, vibrations, light, and geometric shapes, all of which form the essence of every being born in the Divine Source. Without exception, every element that serves the healing and regeneration of the human being is connected to the systems of Divine Consciousness, its intelligence and order. All these technologies were developed specifically to help human beings.

The extraterrestrial civilizations that have long been working to help humanity, and are preparing such technologies, are working together with many other peace-loving civilizations. The cooperation between them takes place in purest love, purest consciousness, and with the purest intention. We too often connect with them, and we are all looking forward to the time when these long-prepared technologies will be handed over to humanity. The way they all work is basically quite simple, and they will bring human beings and their structure back into the original order.

Communication between peace-loving, cosmic human civilizations, the civilizations under Earth's surface, and us takes place, in most cases, via light portals inside Earth. These portals give us the opportunity to visit and communicate with each other physically and in a luminous, subtle form.

It is also possible for us to bring our technologies, which also have their own intelligence and consciousness, to Earth via these portals. These technologies can only be used where they themselves wish to be used and where suitable conditions are in place to ensure their successful utilization with the purest intentions. All these technologies have their own intelligence and mind, whether they were developed by civilizations below Earth's surface or by extraterrestrial peace-loving civilizations. You could say that they are highly developed, luminous vibrating beings, connected with Divine Consciousness, who serve in the purest love. They are not meant to serve people or beings who do not have pure intentions or a pure consciousness, and who do not respect divine laws.

The human community is preparing to connect with the purest consciousness of technologies. Every person aligned physically, mentally, and on the soul level with higher-vibrational levels knows what we are talking about.

You are preparing to connect with their purest, highest fields of consciousness. The time period you are in will enable this connection. It will enable your connection with the purest divine laws and with technologies that fulfill their tasks on the basis of the purest consciousness and in pure love.

With these words we bring you the energy of the purest cosmic energies and cosmic laws, and we are all looking forward to your light-filled future, full of pure, divine light and pure, divine information.

Have trust in this time period. Trust that you are on the right path.

Milin, Rahul, and their Pleiadian companions
Peace with you. Peace with us!

20

Channeling Light Beings
from Earth's Interior

As I was writing about the inner worlds of Mother Earth, I kept feeling that the light beings living there wanted to let us hear their words for the first time. To me, their energy feels a little different than the energy of the light beings of the cosmic world. Their light energy also contains the power of Earth, which accompanies and supports us and lifts us up whenever our energies wane.

I think we will learn a lot more about these noble beings and their life situation in the future. I think their presence and the energy work they do for us will help us to align with the original divine order. We will receive their energy just as we receive energy from the cosmos. Everything will correspond more closely with the natural order once again. I think we have been missing a considerable part of our self that is in connection with these beings. We belong to each other. We were separated from each other. Now, our human systems can begin to connect with the original energy and also to experience the full power of these beings.

I have been communicating with them for some time now. Full of joy and gratitude, I hereby transmit to you the first message from the subtle light beings who live in the luminous dimensions beneath the surface of our Earth.

It is time for us to find each other . . .

Healing Message
Concerning Portal Opening

"We greet you, dear ones, and bring you information from our spaces and dimensions of light!

Light, how wonderful that sounds. The light in our dimensions is similar to the light of the cosmic world. The light from both worlds is mixing.

Borders and barriers are falling. The gates to the world of the cosmos, to the world of cosmic beings, and to human beings have opened.

Even if human timekeeping is irrelevant to us, we are overjoyed that the interior world of Earth is now connecting with the exterior world of Earth. We are overjoyed to be able to bring you frequencies of joy and cheerful gladness with regard to our new, joint future.

We feel the power within ourselves, and we now have the opportunity to pass on our information and frequencies to the human community as well. This information and these frequencies will strengthen the human community and help you in your healing process. The whole of creation on the surface—the animals, the plants, and all natural beings—will be supported by this information.

We bring you light-filled frequencies of love.

Everything will be whole again, everything will be complete. Everything is combining and will become the whole that was once the basis of everything. It will mold itself back to its original shape. Dimensions and spaces are connecting and beginning to create worlds that are inside and outside of your sacred heart space.

In the state of divine order, everything is connected, everything is one.

Our existence brings you waves and codes of love and light. Our existence connects you with the information of the human chronicle—which you are still seeking on the outside, even though you carry it within your heart spaces.

Our existence activates access to these chronicles, enabling you to find them everywhere. As above, so below.

As on the inside, so on the outside.

Our existence helps you to successfully reach the goal of your desired future.

We connect you with the crystals and their systems.

We connect you with the sacred places of this planet. This will increase your awareness.

We activate the chakras of the lower part of your body that connect you with Earth.

We activate the light chakras that are located below your physical body.

We bring you the wisdom and power of Earth.

We bring you information that will help your soul to remember its essence and its past lives—lives in which you have lived in harmony with this planet and in harmony with the cosmic laws.

We help you to free yourselves from the illusion of your perception.

We help you to free yourselves from the illusion of your time.

We help you to free yourselves from the illusion of your thoughts.

We help you to free yourselves from the illusion of your ego.

We help you to find the higher self within your own self.

We help you to connect your outer world with your inner world.

We will bring you information that will flow through your veins like a stream of life and show you our world—full of light, radiant and divine.

The gates to God have been opened.

The gates to God in your heart have been opened.

The gates to understanding your entire existence have been opened.

The gates to yourselves have been opened.

The gates have opened, and they will remain open. Your positive future is assured. For every one of you who chooses a positive future.

We are with you. We are in your hearts. We are in your thoughts."

21

Cosmic Children Are Coming
to You from Distant Worlds

M any of your planet's children belong to a generation that, together with other children who are preparing to incarnate, will be building new systems and new structures of human community. Many of them are already working to create new structures in school systems.

They are involved in protecting and supporting nature. They are participating in the emergence of new organizations that will create new systems based on a natural state of being and a natural foundation.

These children will help your generation by contributing to your world with new and holistic perceptions and insights. Their strong connection with nature gives them the enormous potential to bring a maximum state of naturalness, playfulness, and, above all, respect and love for all living beings on this planet to the most diverse systems of the human community. Many of them belong to the group of children we call cosmic children. Their souls come from cosmic worlds to help planet Earth, its nature and its community, and, as you know, we value them greatly.

Most of these children come from distant galaxies and even distant universes. They are connected with the love of Divine Intelligence and carry the light of the cosmic colors and frequencies of their distant homeland, which open the hearts of the adults and the hearts of all those who are in their vicinity. *These children carry the highest divine love within them.*

Cosmic children often have difficulties anchoring themselves. The luminous frequency of their soul and the luminous composition of their DNA are not yet compatible with the frequencies and spaces in this galaxy and on this planet. They radiate a glowing golden color that shines from their soul, and they often find it difficult to be still. They are constantly searching for the light and its frequencies, wanting to be filled with it. Frequencies in higher dimensions of consciousness are their elixir of life because, for them, they not only contain light-filled information but also light-filled nourishment.

These children's intuition is highly developed and their soul is striving for and looking forward to merging with the spaces of higher consciousness on planet Earth. But until that time comes, many of them will experience health problems in their body sheath, and their soul and mind will often suffer from the lack of light frequencies of love. But they do know how to communicate through telepathy.

The souls of these cosmic children often arrive on this planet in whole groups. The members of these groups know each other, their souls know of each other and they support each other. Especially during sleep, they can connect with each other and pass on knowledge about the most diverse events. They remain connected to their home planet at all times.

The physical beings whose souls come to you on planet Earth are very wise. They are highly developed in terms of consciousness and yet there is playfulness in their souls. You could also say that, even as adults, they remain children in the depths of their souls. They are very slender and youthful in appearance and remain so throughout their lives, even though they live to be thousands of years old.

The community of these beings is divided into a gendered and a genderless one. Physically, they are very similar to human beings. Their genetics are also similar to those of human beings, and they eat a vegan diet. They live in harmony with nature, which is just as beautiful and diverse where they come from as it is on Earth, and they love to connect with animals and other living beings. The technologies they use continually strengthen and regenerate nature. They bring light-filled energy to plants and animals so that everyone on their planet is happy and joyful. They themselves call their world the "Planet of Happiness."

They are very noble beings who honor the laws of light and love.

Normally, the physical beings whose souls come to you as cosmic children rarely travel to planet Earth. They are reluctant to leave their beloved world, where they are completely happy and where they feel connected with all the natural systems. But their code of honor and the request by the Cosmic Council led them to decide to enter a human body, at least for the duration of one human incarnation.

If you can imagine the harmony with nature and with their neighbors they experience in their world, you will certainly understand why the souls of these little human beings, these cosmic children, long for a pure natural world and for the purity of the human soul. You will certainly then realize that the souls of these children living on planet Earth hate conflict because they had only ever lived in joy, lightness, and happiness until the time they left their home planet.

At school on their planet, the souls of these cosmic beings are taught the laws of the cosmos and of resonance, and they are taught cosmic knowledge. They learn to access the cosmic library of knowledge and to "read" its information.

This enables them to extract all the information they need from the morphogenetic fields. They learn to utilize the frequencies of the cosmos for their own personal growth and to develop their healing abilities. They connect with the frequencies of the different colors in order to use them as light nourishment, or as a further source of information, or to regenerate their body or program the crystals they use to heal various systems.

These cosmic children learn telepathy and teleportation at school already. They learn highly developed methods of communication with other beings who have an evolved consciousness on other planets. They learn to communicate with animals and with all forms of animate and inanimate beings. At school, they learn to utilize free energy and manifest it with the help of their thoughts.

Thanks to their high level of consciousness, these beings have multidimensional perception. They can comprehend everything imaginable from several angles and perspectives simultaneously. When they look at a house, they also see the space under the house, behind the house, and above the roof. They can see all the rooms inside the house. They can also immediately see the structure of the materials out of which the house is built. They can instantly communicate with the subtle beings in the house. They can feel the energy that fills the house. They comprehend the entire history of this house. They are also able to perceive situations from several perspectives at the same time; not only from their own perspective, but also from the perspectives of other people or beings who are involved in the situation in some way. They can literally see other people's thoughts and emotions with regard to the situation and clearly read their intentions.

This ability is practiced with the children at school on their home planet, enabling them to truly perfect their personality. The aim of these lessons is to understand another person in love, and to fully comprehend another person's view of a particular matter or situation.

And many beings who are at home on the "Planet of Happiness" have, at the request of the Cosmic Council, taken on the honorable task of descending into the low-vibrational 3D levels of planet Earth and helping the human community to accelerate its evolution of consciousness.

Sometimes these beings want to waste no time, so they incarnate immediately into the body of a fetus on the common timeline. Often, however, they first embark on a journey through time, and incarnate into the human community at a different time that is precisely calculated and determined, usually in large cities where it is not possible to detect their origin. As soon as their age allows them to do so, they begin, while still quite young, to act and take steps to support the human community and planet Earth.

Before they incarnate among you, they link themselves to the field of language and to the information fields of the respective community so that they can fit in and immediately start to work.

We share all of this with you in the hope that it will help parents of cosmic children. Perhaps this will help the parents of these children to better understand their behavior and their outrage at the state of the human community. Perhaps this will help them to better understand how evolved and wise the soul of their child really is and from which cosmic world they come.

In any case, the souls of these children usually choose parents who they are sure will support them in spreading their knowledge and light here on Earth.

The parents of these children often wonder why their child seems to be so different and does not seem to resemble anyone else in the family.

But they themselves have a good understanding of their child and feel deeply bonded. From the very beginning, these children need protection on the energy level for their earthly existence and development. In adulthood they then transfer their energy to their parents, supporting them in turn. This creates an ever-deepening sense of closeness.

Many of these children also take on another task: they create the energetic conditions for the arrival of extraterrestrial civilizations.

They will then, in due course, act as "interpreters" in meetings between other civilizations arriving on Earth and the human community.

Many of these children only choose to have one or at most two incarnations on planet Earth. After leaving their bodies, most will return directly to their home world, to their original bodies, to their original age, and to their original family or relations, to the surroundings they left when they came to Earth. A cosmic family merely "lends" the soul of any of its members to humanity for a certain time to help in its transition to higher spheres. On their planet, the world from which the cosmic child's soul comes, time does not pass as it does on planet Earth.

Their absence is therefore not too lengthy.

Let us allow the souls of these honorable beings to unfold their loving and helpful influence among you on Earth, and let us send them the love of our hearts.

Let us bless their honorable intention and the mission for which they have chosen to come.

Let us bless their existence on the Earth.

Let us bless them on all levels of their being.

In love and peace for this planet, for human beings and their future!

Orin and his Pleiadian companions
Peace with you. Peace with us!

22

The Energy of Our Words
Connects You with Us and Increases
Your Light and Consciousness

The long absence of love on planet Earth has sickened many of the systems of the human community. It has sickened many human souls and many human hearts. During the current time period, everything in your world will return to its original order. Everything will return to its original natural state.

This book supports you with the frequency of love. We have programmed every word in it with the frequency of love. This is how we have connected you with love and ensured that the love of the Divine Source flows to you. The love in your heart connects you with cosmic freedom and all its divine values.

We know that your light-filled frequency of love is forming an ever-stronger connection with us and that it will not be long before we can live in these frequencies together.

We know that telepathic communication between us is deepening with each new day.

It is a great honor for us to see how quickly this development is progressing, and how many thousands and thousands of people are already connecting with us thanks to the words Pavlina receives from us. It is an infinite honor to connect with you, the readers and supporters of Pleiadian messages. This connection is formed as each word is read. Your systems of soul, mind, and body, as well as your energy body, will shine in beautifully radiant colors. To us, you look like a glittering sea of stars populating your planet.

The radiance that emanates from you when you read and connect opens the door to those most diverse dimensions and spaces that connect you people of good will with each other.

Essentially, everything is one whole. The light connects us. And the luminous radiance you generate when you commune with us forms connections between all of us and allows us to become a huge community of light.

When you read our words, which Pavlina has "translated" into your human language, your consciousness increases, it expands into the most diverse spaces of your being and connects with your higher consciousness—with your higher self. Your higher consciousness connects you with the light beings who are responsible for you. From your higher consciousness, you constantly receive light-filled impulses and information that come from the intelligence of Divine Consciousness and from your light beings, who are in constant contact with your higher consciousness.

When we observe you readers from our perspective, we see a glittering light streaming from higher spaces toward you—stars on Earth. It permeates the systems of your soul, mind, body, and energy bodies. A beautiful sparkling flow of knowledge is permeating your systems, bringing information to raise your personal light vibration and knowledge. It brings information from the worlds of the Divine Infinite Source.

Your intention to connect with the world of light and its beings is enough to bind you to the world of light and its beings. We see that, when you connect, you are in your own light-filled reality. You are surrounded by an infinite number of light beings who love you infinitely. Each of you is in your own luminous world, which, for each of you, constitutes your personal reality.

It is a great honor for us to touch you with light in such moments.

How glad we are to see that your life is changing so positively and that your light beings, together with your higher self, are guiding you. It is beautiful to see that, thanks to reading these words, those of you who may have previously lived in solitude and been somewhat disconnected from the world of light are now surrounded by light beings. There are light beings around you—right at this moment. They are in your immediate vicinity.

They accompany you. They connect with your emotions. They love you more than anything. They watch over you and guard you . . .

And their conscious and declared intention is to help you on your path. Their greatest wish is to see you joyful.

Right now, they are touching you with light. They connect with your heart and with the love you carry in your heart. Love binds you together.

The light and love that are constantly growing within you create a bond of light, love, gratitude, and happiness between you and your light beings. And this light-filled bond between you links you to the world of the cosmos.

It is also our greatest wish to see you joyful and free in your soul and in your thinking.

That is our greatest wish and the goal of the journey we have been on with Pavlina since 2016. Since that year, we have been accompanying you assertedly and explicitly, and you have made enormous progress in your thinking, in your perception, in your healing of reality, in your development of consciousness—and not least in your liberation.

We are very grateful for this development. We are very grateful that we have already come so far in the task we have set ourselves. Because it is our task, accompanied by divine love, to help you gain happiness and the freedom of your soul and mind, and the freedom of your earthly reality.

Every human being who takes steps toward happiness and personal freedom causes us immeasurable joy. We celebrate it here in our realms. We rejoice over every human being, truly every individual who, thanks to our information, walks the path to light, love, and freedom, no matter how small their steps were or are. The only thing that matters is that they have decided to walk this path.

We thank each and every one of you. Our gratitude accompanies you. We thank every individual for raising the light of our collective light-filled community. Because, as you probably know, we are all one big, infinite, common whole. And we support each other.

We send you the love of our hearts.

Affirmation of love

Here is another affirmation for you. It will accompany you on your path. It connects you with the love of the Divine Source, with the love of all light beings, with the love of all loving beings, and with the love that you yourselves carry within your heart.

It is best to speak this affirmation out loud and very consciously. With every word spoken, you will feel that the love within you and the love that flows out of you is expanding into all spaces of your being and life and connecting you with everything that is essential to you.

Affirmation of Love

"I am the love of the Divine Source.
I am infinite love, connected with everything loving.
The love of my heart connects me with everything divine.
The love of my heart connects me with everything that is peaceful and light-filled.
I AM LOVE."

Your Pleiadian companions Orella,
Vilalata, Milin, Ramuel, Rahul, Wahou
Peace with you. Peace with us!

23

Phenomena of the Current Time
and Tips for Leaving the
Third Dimension of Consciousness

In your present incarnation you are increasingly detaching yourselves from the fields of illusion. One of the illusions you are still under is the assumption that you are moving around on a globe, on a spherical world. Your perception of this illusion dictates this to you, causing you to believe it. However, the low-vibrational, virtual three-dimensional space in which you move is a flat, closed plane.

We are not saying that the world is not spherical. It is spherical. But what you perceive of it, within the illusion, is a suggestion. It is a different globe to the one you really live on. And to experience this truth, you must rise out of the fields of illusion and connect with the true reality of Earth, which moves, beautifully radiant and spherical, in the vastness of the universe. Only when you step out of the fields of this illusion will you no longer move on the closed, three-dimensional plane, which imprisons you in its space and time and does not allow you to grow. It does not allow your consciousness to connect with the higher spaces and dimensions.

The illusionary dimension of the third level of consciousness is separated within its time period from the true reality of Earth.

You should know: like yourselves, your Earth is a multidimensional being. She is also striving toward her own light and her divine reality. Divine Intelligence is currently neutralizing those energetic imprints of Earth that no longer serve anyone and that vibrate at a low level. It is neutralizing an infinite number of imprints that connect Earth and its population with the negative past.

Many of you have already separated yourselves to a considerable degree from the fields of illusion, or are in the process of separating yourselves from them. Through this, you are at least partially connected with the true reality of Earth and its higher levels. You are able to free yourselves from the low-vibrational third dimension of consciousness by expanding your consciousness and by finding the light within your heart, as well as by finding love for yourselves and love for your neighbors.

However, your separation from the low-vibrational 3D plane allows you to experience a wide variety of phenomena that were previously unknown to you.

This can lead to situations that catch you off guard. When you connect to the spaces of higher consciousness and disconnect from the lower-vibrational 3D planes of illusion, the energetic bonds between you and the higher dimensions break, and you find yourself in a space that is, in a sense, between dimensions. Surprising irregularities can therefore occur in various areas of your system, which you should be prepared for.

Your body may lose stability. Then it may be that, for seemingly inexplicable reasons, you slip or have an accident and feel as if your body is in an empty space no longer subject to the physical gravitational pull of Earth. A weakening of the nervous system and an instability of the digestive system are also typical, because your digestive organs are located in the center of your body, connecting you with Earth as well as with the cosmos. And the temporary disharmony of the in-between space has a very strong effect on them.

Your mind, which is doing more work during this time, is often in this in-between space too. It may seem to disconnect from your brain and your personality. This could manifest in memory loss. It could be that you frequently search in vain for words, in completely normal, everyday situations, or are more forgetful than usual. You may not be able to concentrate. Your dreams and sleeping style may have changed as your mind is not so often present and not always connected with you.

You may sometimes find yourself in situations that seem absurd and pointless. Or some mishap may occur and afterwards you cannot account for it and have the feeling you were mentally not even present during the incident. Or you may have the impression that you are observing situations from the perspective of a stranger, or are merely an observer of a situation. It is also possible that your electrical or energy devices lose their stability. They were not designed for the vibrations of higher, luminous dimensions of consciousness, so they are incompatible with these high-vibrational frequencies. The influx of high-vibrational, light-filled frequencies into the plane of the 3D illusion will shake up a wide variety of the systems of human beings and their homes. Many systems will collapse because of this and no longer work.

We would of course like to support you and give you a few tips that can help you during this time of transition into the higher, luminous dimensions.

Tips for Maintaining Your Stability and for an Easier Departure from the Intermediate Space into Higher Dimensions of Consciousness

Earlier in this book we gave you the Earth symbol, which we had programmed. This healing sign can be of great benefit to you at this time, because it helps to maintain your stability. It connects you with the true reality of Earth and with her natural light matrix. It connects you with Earth's purest order. It connects you with the true spherical shape of your Earth. It helps you to separate yourself from the lower-vibrational levels.

The number sequence **33851651** also helps you to detach yourself more easily from the 3D plane, and, last but not least, it supports you in the transition to 5D. Thanks to this number sequence, you can anchor yourself more easily in the new dimensions of consciousness. It also helps you to free yourself from the remaining elements of your ego that no longer serve you. At the same time, it neutralizes the energetic imprints of your personal negative past and the negative past of previous incarnations.

Use the number sequence **8787** to connect with everything pure that belongs to human beings and that human beings carry within themselves. It connects you with the purest essence of the morphogenetic fields of humanity, helping you to find your own purest core. This is achieved through connecting with the purest crystalline frequencies of the universe, which heal your heart and connect you to the natural crystal matrix of your galaxy and planet.

The number sequence **34345781**, from *Pleiadian Soul Healing*, enables you to remember the purest essence of your soul. It also protects the light of your soul. It reminds you of the task you set yourself for this incarnation. Since you wanted to work as a light worker, it activates your healing abilities.

The number sequence **57819**, also from *Pleiadian Soul Healing*, helps you to neutralize negative programs, memories, and visions from the past that no longer serve you or that have arisen through the manipulation of humanity.

The number series **4374**, which we gave you in *Light Messages from the Pleiades*, helps you purify, heal, and regenerate your DNA. It supports the removal of harmful substances, and any side effects caused by medication, from your body.

Connect to the Cosmic Healing Pharmacy, which we first introduced to you in *Light Messages from the Pleiades*. In the Healing Pharmacy you will find all the subtle preparations that can heal and regenerate your body, mind, and soul. The light beings who energetically stock this Healing Pharmacy for you give you the exact preparations, frequencies, colors, sounds, and geometric shapes that you need at any one moment and that support you in these challenging times.

Use the geometric form of the Flower of Life. Its form connects you with the signature of the universe and with the signature of divine happening. It connects you with your original divine signature, which consists of circles of light. The shape of the Flower of Life connects you with the consciousness database of the cosmos, which contains Divine Consciousness and all the information of Divine Intelligence. It connects you with all the light-filled and loving times and spaces of the universe. The places or points where the circles intersect are entrances to other dimensions and light-filled spaces. The shape of the Flower of Life connects you with the sacred chamber of your heart and brings you infinite possibilities for your being and your life. The Flower of Life protects you from external energetic influences.

Meditative Connection with the Flower of Life

Breathe deeply and concentrate on your heart.

Look inside your heart, inside your heart organ.

See whether your heart is radiant. If it is not, allow your heart organ to lighten up and see how it now shines like a sun.

This light penetrates every cell.

It radiates through your whole body.

Be simply with yourself in this moment. You are the most important person, and, through your own healing, you also heal your loved ones and your environment.

Concentrate only on yourself and on the purity of your heart and thoughts.

Breathe deeply and, with each exhalation, let go of worries and thoughts that are weighing you down.

Now, return to your heart, which is shining like a beautiful sun and whose rays are lighting up your entire body.

Observe how your entire body is radiating. This clear light penetrates your entire aura.

Your light is so powerful. You radiate love in every direction of your existence.

Now imagine the Flower of Life. Imagine it spatially, in 3D. It is a flexible, huge sphere.

Now place yourself inside this Flower of Life, in its very center—place its center in your heart.

Now imagine the Flower of Life. Imagine it spatially, in 3D. It is a flexible, huge sphere.

Now place yourself inside this Flower of Life, in its very center—place its center in your heart.

Increase the intensity of your loving heart light, and, with your heart, illuminate all the structures of this beautiful sphere.

You are completely connected with the original code and the signature of the universe. You are absolutely united with the divine order. Your connection with the Flower of Life harmonizes you and protects you energetically.

Breathe deeply and realize the power of your connection with the universe and therefore your connection with yourself.

If you wish to strengthen your connection with the divine signature even more, visualize how this flexible Flower of Life expands in its structure into infinity—with you at its center.

Bless yourself on all levels of your existence.

However, there are other possibilities for an easier departure from the intermediate space into higher dimensions of consciousness, which we have occasionally given you in the form of important tips and exercises in the course of our messages. The following aids can also help to make the influx of high-vibrational, light-filled frequencies into the level of the 3D illusion more bearable . . .

Further Tips and Advice for Your Stability

Practice forgiveness. This is a major factor in being able to leave low-vibrational levels. Forgive yourself, forgive others, and ask others for forgiveness. Forgiveness carried out at the soul level also brings freedom and health on all levels of your being, and new positive energy.

Let go of emotions and thoughts of unnatural fear. Fear binds the energy of your heart and closes the sacred chamber of your heart. Unnatural fear is the most burdensome emotion imposed upon humankind by the dark forces.

Think positive. Bless thoughts that are not your own and that bind you. Blessing transforms them into a luminous form. You can also ask negative thoughts to leave you and return to their source. Simply do not allow them to return to you. Thoughts are intelligent and able to understand your intention. Negative thought forms have no right to approach you and interfere with your free will unless you allow them to.

Control your thoughts. Don't talk nastily or maliciously about others. Try to see the purest essence of every person and being you encounter, regardless of the circumstances. Always remember that you are connected by the purest essence.

Act according to the law of resonance. Everything you think and do has consequences. Therefore, attract into your life only that which is truly positive and loving.

Feel gratitude in your heart. Gratitude connects you with your light companions and opens up access to all the light-filled, loving spaces and times of the universe. Gratitude activates the sacred chamber of your heart.

Meditate. No matter what kind of meditation you do—whether you meditate sitting up, lying down, or walking, with or without music—unify your soul, your mind, and your body during meditation. Your heart thereby opens a light portal to the light worlds and their beings.

Go out into nature as often as you can. Nature is the best healer, so spend time with her as often as possible. The sun brings you light-filled information for the development of your DNA and for the development of your consciousness. The element of water also helps you to regenerate, heal, and purify your DNA. Nature beings purify your mind, soul, and body.

Eat a supportive diet. Try to eat light and healthy food that does not upset your energy levels. Drink plenty of good-quality water.

Find the love within you again. Start by appreciating yourself. Your self-love unites you with the love of the Divine Source and with everything loving that surrounds you.

Let the Energy of the New Era Enter in

Rid yourself of burdensome things that bind your energy, pass on any objects in your household that no longer serve you or bring you joy. Also remove any objects that drain your life energy and lower the energy of your home. Let your home breathe freely again. Tidy up those areas in your flat or house where you feel the energy to be "stagnant" or blocked.

Become aware of objects that connect you to bad thoughts and memories, or to the low-vibrational energy of the 3D plane, and remove them. You will notice that your soul, mind, and body feel lighter.

Let the energy of the New Era, which is already connecting with all of your systems, enter your home. Give it space by getting rid of objects that carry burdensome and "old" energies.

There are endless tips and advice that we could list. But, as we have often said, the most important thing is to form an intention, whether that concerns positive development, your healing process, or anything else. An intention is a ray of light emanating from your system. And this ray of light opens up spaces, times, and dimensions for the fulfillment of your wish.

Be happy, rejoice, dance, become a joyful little child again, living in the here and now. Your joy and bliss will be reflected in the spaces of the light worlds where these delightful properties exist. Your light companions and the world around you—the earthly world and the light world—rejoice with you.

And we are also delighted that we were allowed to accompany and help you once more. We thank you all for your interest and for your heartfelt love.

Milin and his Pleiadian companions
Peace with you. Peace with us!

24

Stepping Out of Low-Vibrational Dimensions Through the Expansion of Your Consciousness

We have already mentioned several times that you will be able to step out of lower-vibrational dimensions by expanding your consciousness. For your further support, we would now like to give you an affirmation that can help you develop and expand your consciousness. This affirmation will make it easier for you to step out of low vibrations. It will make it easier for you to move around in 5D.

This affirmation enables you to connect with your higher consciousness and your higher intelligence. Your soul expands its light and unites with the frequency of cosmic freedom. Your mind unites with positive beings and beings of good will. Your body unites with cosmic colors and merges with the divine order.

When you speak this affirmation, the frequency of divine knowledge and consciousness can flow to you freely. The knowledge stream of divine freedom then brings you information that connects you with the knowledge of infinite Divine Intelligence. This activates the power that is hidden in the sacred chamber of your heart. Step by step, you begin to look at earthly situations from a higher perspective, you begin to understand the complexity of earthly and cosmic events. With our love and with divine love, we have programmed the following affirmation to facilitate departure from low-vibrational dimensions. It is programmed with positive frequencies and cosmic colors that help you transform the individual words of the affirmation as you speak them into positive energetic imprints pertaining to your reality.

Every word of this affirmation has its own specific vibration that anchors itself in your system.

Every word of this affirmation brings you clarity and the determination to release low-vibrational realities and leave them behind you.

Be aware that after working with this affirmation, negative programs, as well as human beings or other beings that burden you, will most likely say goodbye. Be aware of this.

Only use this affirmation if you are truly ready for detachment from all negativity and are prepared for this detachment to induce change. Be aware that the light guides who are in your immediate vicinity will see and hear your every word and bring positive change to you.

We wish you much strength and success on your new, earthly path, full of light and love.

Affirmation for Stepping Out of Low-Vibrational Dimensions

"I [your first name] call on all light guides who are responsible for my existence. I connect with them through the power of my love, my gratitude, and my purest intention. I ask all my light guides for help and for my intention to be heard.

Now and in this space, I, [your first name], choose to step out of the lower-vibrational dimensions of my reality.

My decision stands firm and is in harmony with my free will and my consciousness. My decision is in harmony with the divine order.

Now and in this space, I choose to release all low-vibrational burdens that prevent me from developing my consciousness. Now and in this space, I choose to free my soul, my mind, my body, and my energy body from all low-vibrational burdens.

Now and in this space, I choose to leave the reality of lower-vibrational dimensions.

Here and now, I choose to ascend into the higher, light-filled spaces of consciousness and to unite with my higher consciousness and my higher intelligence.

My intention is clear and pure.

My intention connects me in the here and now with the divine order, with Divine Consciousness, with divine love, with divine light, and with all elements of the Divine Source.

My heart is filled with love, light, and gratitude.

My heart unites me with all that is loving and light-filled in this and all other worlds.

My soul, my mind, my body, and my energy body are bonded with cosmic freedom in the here and now.

I am free in the here and now."

With love and peace in our hearts!
Your Pleiadian companions

25

Cosmic Color Beings, the Properties of Colors, and an Exercise in Making Contact

Each cosmic color has its own frequencies, its own light, its own information, its own cosmic tones, and its own geometric shapes.

Each cosmic color supports you with its specific, individual properties. And, at the same time, these individual colors complement each other and together form a single, huge, cosmic element. Each of these colors is unique and each of these colors is instrumental in helping the whole, infinite happening of the infinite universe to unfold in its greatness and uniqueness.

These cosmic colors help in the creation and development of new forms of life and new forms of existence. They help to regenerate, they help to heal, and they ensure that the consciousness of a being can develop.

Every being in a physical body bonds with the multitudinous colors of the Divine Source. Such a being uses these cosmic colors for its own existence and life in particular places or on particular planets in this infinite universe. It uses these colors with light-filled intention and allows their frequencies to flow into its physical and subtle body.

Every human being is also connected with the color frequencies of the Divine Source. Even if not everyone is aware of it, cosmic colors influence the life, the life situations, and the bodily functions of every single person.

Every human being absorbs the colors of the Divine Source that nourish and regenerate them, and every human being has brought to this planet their own special connection that is unique to them and that manifests itself as physical vibrations of light.

These light vibrations, these cosmic color frequencies, permeate their aura and form the basic, dominant colors of their energy body. They also penetrate their chakras, and they penetrate their organs and body systems. Their organs then vibrate in harmony with these cosmic color frequencies and the frequencies of the surrounding planets. Their chakras form a colorful and light-filled connection with the chakras of the universe.

The color spectrum that forms around every human being permeates their soul and mind. It connects them in this way with the richness and variety of colors of the universe. Under normal circumstances—and by this we mean being in connection with the universe and Earth simultaneously—human beings are able to completely regenerate themselves and perfectly absorb the cosmic colors into their systems.

Through past manipulation, human beings have unfortunately been partially cut off from the color diversity of the universe—however, through gradually stepping out of the lower-vibrational levels, their opportunities to connect with the healing and rejuvenating properties of color are increasing.

The human body is becoming increasingly more subtle, chakras are becoming more luminous, and meridians are connecting with the systems of the universe. The crystalline systems of human beings absorb the crystalline frequencies of the universe and ensure their connection with the crystal frequencies of the higher realms of consciousness. In the future, thanks to this development, human beings will once again be able to make greater use of the healing and regenerative properties of cosmic colors.

There is a specific cosmic light being responsible for each cosmic color. These are subtle beings who act as luminous guardians throughout the universe. These light beings work in harmony with the Divine Source and with the divine order. They are located in divine space and work together with those subtle light beings who are responsible for the individual planets.

The light beings of the cosmic colors are connected with Divine Intelligence through their consciousness.

In a figurative sense, you could therefore say that every color carries a part of Divine Consciousness and Divine Intelligence. And every color comes to you directly from the Divine Source.

Properties of the cosmic primary colors

We would like to describe some important properties of the cosmic primary colors from a spiritual perspective. There are, of course, countless color nuances and shades. There are also colors that you cannot yet perceive with your human sense of sight because your brain has not yet adjusted to them. That is why we will now describe some of the basic cosmic colors. We will then help you to make contact with the light beings of the relevant colors through a simple exercise and affirmation.

1. **Cosmic color WHITE:** This connects you with the purity, wisdom, and peace of the universe. It is strongly connected with the "stillness" of the universe, and helps your physical body to alleviate pain.

2. **Cosmic color PINK:** This color brings love—the love of the Divine Source. It ensures that you develop self-love and connect with everything loving. It is the "main activator" of gratitude in your heart. This color brings a natural, cosmic feminine power. Just like the color gold, it brings the highest consciousness of love from the Divine Source. Small babies are very strongly associated with pink when they arrive on planet Earth. The love of the Divine Source is a frequency that is able to heal every negative program and burden that human beings carry with them, provided they allow themselves to be healed.

3. **Cosmic color YELLOW:** Yellow is a color that radiates through your entire system and supports it in connecting with other cosmic colors. It acts as an amplifier for the reception of the other cosmic colors and is connected

with the original divine frequency of the sun in your planetary system. Just like the color gold, yellow supports the unfolding of your DNA. It connects you with your intuition. Children love this color because it reminds them of the joy that fills the Divine Source. Most animals living in the wild also love it.

4. **Cosmic color ORANGE:** This color is the inspiration of Divine Intelligence. It brings you creativity and a connection with your original creative qualities. It also brings you new ideas and inspiration. It brings playfulness, cheerfulness, and at the same time a feeling of security.

5. **Cosmic color RED:** Above all, red brings the power of the universe to your body. It brings life energy to your body and supports it in receiving other color frequencies. Red is the color of manifestation. Just like orange, red is the color of the intention you send out from your system before the manifestation or visualization of your desire. Red is the color of your determination and turns your thoughts into reality. This color helps your mind to free itself from negative programs.

6. **Cosmic color LIGHT BLUE:** Light blue brings relaxation to your physical body. It brings you the natural, cosmic masculine power and the magic of the universe. This color supports your mind in its development of consciousness. It connects you with the element of water on planet Earth and it brings "cooling" to your body in case you experience feverish conditions and inflammations.

7. **Cosmic color DARK BLUE/INDIGO:** This is the color of God. Just like gold, it generates a ray of divine knowledge, divine power, and omnipotent action. Human beings are connected to this color via their third eye, which receives

information concerning divine knowledge and infinite divine happenings. It helps to develop telepathy and intuition.

8. **Cosmic color GREEN:** This color is used for healing. Above all, it heals your soul. It helps your soul to expand its consciousness and thereby connect with other beings of evolved consciousness. At the same time, it calms your soul. With the help of this color, your soul can free itself from foreign emotions. Green also helps to heal your body. It connects you with the color of your forests and nature, thereby strengthening the healing effect of natural elements and frequencies.

9. **Cosmic color LILAC:** This color helps with the transformation of any negative issues, It purifies your aura and all of the sections and areas of your energetic body. The frequency of this color allows you to transition more easily into higher realms of consciousness. Just like the cosmic color gold, this color therefore acts as an energetic "bridge" to the new, positive systems of your future.

10. **Cosmic color SILVER:** Silver purifies and neutralizes any negativity that has accumulated in your cells or body systems. It cools and has an anti-inflammatory effect. In energy work, it is also very helpful in mirroring energies, if you have the impression that you need special protection or are exposed to attacks. Silver renders you invisible to negative energies or beings. As this frequency is capable of excellent communication with the magnetic laws of the universe, the domain of silver also includes technical achievements in highly developed cosmic civilizations. Just like the color gold, silver emphasizes divine omnipotence. Together they form the "river of knowledge" that flows from the Divine Source to you—a

beautiful stream whose waves are made up of sparkling particles. The color silver is also associated with immensely luminous beings of the fifth and seventh dimensions of consciousness. It is a precursor of the color gold, which, from a spiritual point of view, is the highest frequency of consciousness of the Divine Source, and an inspiration for new life forms that arise in the Divine Source. We perceive the color silver as a counterpart to the color gold. Both complement each other and often work together. The color silver is the "cosmic partner" of the color gold.

11. **Cosmic color GOLD:** This color brings connection with the Divine Source and with absolutely all of its properties. Gold is the color of the origin of cosmic life and the symbolism of cosmic life. It brings the highest spirituality and connection with the cosmic consciousness of Christ energy and symbolizes the brilliance and radiance of the universe, its infinite beauty, and its infinite happenings. Gold permeates all beings of these infinite cosmic happenings. It is the color of creation and passing away, although nothing every really passes away. Passing away simply means transition or birth into a new form. The color gold connects you with the infinite diversity and multidimensionality of the universe.

   Through this color, the essence of every being is connected with the Divine Source, their divine home. Even those beings who have chosen something other than the positive development of their existence bear traces of a golden connection with the Divine Source. This connection through the color gold, no matter how weak, ensures that beings who are not so light-filled will one day remember the divine light within them. Under optimal circumstances, the color gold nourishes your entire system. Once you choose your personal light body process, you will find that the color gold spreads throughout your systems.

During the light body process, every cell in your body
connects with this golden frequency and lets its light shine.

12. **Cosmic color CRYSTAL:** The crystalline, transparent
frequency is found everywhere in the universe. It brings
you connection with the purest systems of the divine.
It connects you with the consciousness database of the
universe and brings crystalline light information to all
your systems, your cells, and your DNA, helping you
to expand your consciousness. The crystalline cosmic
frequency permeates all of the systems of your body and
creates crystal structures within you that connect you with
the crystal structures of your galaxy and planet Earth. This
crystal frequency heals the hearts of human beings with its
incomparable light and frees them of all low-vibrational
emotions. It brings the hearts of human beings the purity
they long for, connecting them with the purest essence of
their wonderful soul.

13. **Cosmic color BROWN, SHIMMERING:** The color brown
is not one of the primary colors. However, by mixing
different hues, this frequency flows into your body as
a shimmering brown. The intelligence of your body
loves brown because it receives strength through the
connection this color provides with the element of wood
and with Earth herself. Brown helps it to connect with
the naturalness of the planet. This color has a calming and
grounding effect on your body.

14. **Cosmic color BLACK:** Black is actually the color of
"night." This color, which is not truly a color in the
physical sense, can be found wherever there is no light.
This "night" color helps your system to become calm and
relaxed. It helps all beings and all existences of life to find
light within themselves.

Fundamentally, all cosmic colors and the color nuances of the cosmic colors communicate with each other and bring life energy, consciousness development, and connection with the universe to all other beings in this universe. Even though each cosmic color has its own specific properties, these beings love and honor each other. The light beings of the cosmic colors love you as well.

After consulting with your personal light companions, they will gladly come to you and, with the support of Divine Intelligence, help you move into divine order. If you have the feeling that you need more of a particular cosmic color, you can connect with the corresponding color frequency or the light beings of that color and ask them for help.

You can also make use of the frequency of this color by wearing clothes of the color that you intuitively feel you need most right now. Or you can program water with the corresponding color and then drink it in sips. To do this, place a glass of water on a correspondingly colored piece of paper for at least three minutes. After three minutes, the water will be filled with the frequency of this color.

Contacting Cosmic Color Beings

If you wish to contact the beings of a certain color frequency, you can do the following simple exercise with its affirmation. To do this, make yourself comfortable and breathe deeply.

Let your heart shine with light. Feel gratitude in your heart.

In the here and now, send out a ray of intention from your heart and connect with the cosmic beings of the color you have chosen.

And now say out loud . . .

"The gratitude of my heart connects me with the light beings and the intelligence of the cosmic color [e.g., white].

I ask the intelligence and frequency of the [e.g., white] cosmic color to enter my system. I ask the intelligence and frequency of the [e.g., white] cosmic color to work in my system, thereby providing me with healing and regeneration. In the here and now, my overall system is receiving the intelligence and frequency of the cosmic color [e.g., white].

My overall system is connected with the divine order of colors. Thank you, thank you, thank you."

Ramuel and his Pleiadian companions
Peace with you. Peace with us!

26

The Light Beings of Higher Dimensions of Consciousness Are Already Waiting to Connect with You

If you work on the energetic level with cosmic colors, or connect with cosmic colors during your time in nature, you will find that your whole system rejoices in the newly created, positive energy.

Your organs are remembering their connection with planet Earth and are therefore beginning to reconnect with the energetic frequencies of the solar system. Your body is remembering that it is part of the entire universe. Your mind is remembering its affinity with the human races of the galactic worlds, and your soul is joining its light with all the light-filled frequencies and beings of the cosmos.

The elements that planet Earth is so generously and abundantly filled with—water, earth, fire, and air—will be able to connect with you more easily and communicate and cooperate with you more directly. At the same time, the light beings assigned to these elements will be able to provide you with more of their positive qualities. You will become more visible to them.

As an example of the abundance of light beings accompanying you on your spiritual path, we would like to introduce you to the work of five archangels.

For the elements water, earth, fire, and air, with which you will now be connecting more and more easily and naturally, they are of the greatest significance.

~~~

Archangel Gabriel, who is responsible for the element of water, is regarded as being the angel of proclamation and revelation. He is the bearer of messages and the explainer of visions and is primarily concerned with the energization of river sources. He ensures that the quality of the water is as high as possible. Together with other luminous and cosmic beings, he enriches the water in large lakes, seas, and oceans with oxygen. However, he energizes not only the water on this planet but also the fluids in your body. For you, this makes him one of the most important light beings, because he thereby activates the light-filled information in the human DNA, which initiates healing, purification, and regenerative processes within you. We have already expressed this in our message about the new, natural matrix system of galactic order, which you can read about in *Light Messages from the Pleiades.* Human beings being able to take the first steps toward the expanded development of consciousness and to reconnect all their DNA strands was only made possible by this activation. Through this water-related energy, he is also present in the unborn child during pregnancy and transfers his energy to the amniotic fluid of the child. He is also responsible for the occurrence of rain and snow—we refer to unmanipulated, naturally occurring rain and snow.

~~~

Archangel Uriel is the patron saint of the element of earth and the angel of manifestation. He nourishes the earth energetically, providing harvest and abundance to human beings and all other beings on this planet He helps to energize the energy pathways beneath Earth's surface, and, together with other cosmic powers, he activates the sacred places of this planet and is in constant communication with Gaia. He also supports her in her own ascent to higher dimensions. He works together with light-filled, cosmic frequencies that facilitate an increase in earthly vibration. At the same time, he helps planet Earth to cleanse herself of negative energetic imprints from the past. And he helps you human beings to connect energetically with the element of earth for better grounding.

―――

Archangel Michael is responsible for the element of fire on this planet. Every time you light a fire and enjoy its warmth and naturalness, an energetic contact between you and Archangel Michael is formed. Even if you are simply looking at a flickering candle flame, you are in contact with this archangel and his element. Fire brings you purification, transformation, and a new, pure energy. Archangel Michael uses his fire energy to transform everything that no longer has a place on this planet, including everything negative that is not your own, such as manipulative programs. It is also within his sphere of activity to use his fiery power to transform everything that is not in harmony with justice. He stands up for the weak. He ignites an imaginary flame in people who are enthusiastic about new projects or new ideas. He connects planet Earth with the magical light of the universe.

―――

Archangel Raphael is responsible for the element of air on this planet, not only in the form of the wind, which carries all negativity away from you and purifies your systems, but also in the form of oxygen, which he energizes before you take it into your lungs. Raphael, together with Gabriel and Michael, is considered to be one of the most important archangels, and is known above all as a healer who helps to transport the oxygen you breathe into all areas of your body, no matter how small. He works together with a large number of light beings who are also responsible for the element of air. Take a deep breath and realize that this powerful being of light is with you energetically every time you breathe in. The moment you, as a newborn baby, breathed in for the first time, Archangel Raphael was there to assist you and connect you with the element of air.

Archangel Metatron is the main patron for planet Earth and the highest light being responsible for helping and accompanying humanity in the luminous dimensions of consciousness. People worship him as the crown of creation and the angel of the New Era. He was chosen by Divine Intelligence and the interplanetary Cosmic Council and acts in accordance with their instructions, to which he strictly adheres. In consultation with Divine Intelligence and the interplanetary Cosmic Council, he brings light beings to the planet to help humanity in the various areas and levels of its development. He watches over all light beings on planet Earth, the development of planet Earth, and the development of humanity. He has connections to all dimensions. He is only permitted to help humanity with the approval of the authorities already mentioned. This is because Divine Intelligence always waits for humanity to reach a certain level of consciousness before sending out light beings to support the human community or individual people working behind the scenes. He is also responsible for the Akashic Records, in which all the events of humanity's past are stored.

These archangels and an infinite number of other light beings will be closely accompanying you on your earthly path. And, due to your spiritual development and your connections with the cosmic world and its beautiful colors and frequencies, you are now becoming more visible, day by day, to every positive light being.

Your systems will vibrate with ever more light in the frequency of your planetary system. And your luminous companions, who are constantly with you and watch over you, are delighted with the colorfulness of your systems.

They love every single color and its properties.

They love their expression and they love their ability to expand and connect with the variety of colors and wealth of nuances in the cosmos.

143

They love colors because for them colors are an expression of divine infinity.

Your guardian angels and light companions are the light beings who are closest to you in your personal reality. They love you unconditionally and remind you of the divinity of the universe through their mere presence.

Over time, and as your consciousness evolves, you will merge with the colors of the universe. Your light companions will accompany you on this luminous path. You will merge with the beingness and the happenings that fill this boundless and beautiful universe.

As soon as this takes place, you will realize how much you have been cut off from this infinite, multifaceted happening. You will realize how much strength and how much energy has been taken from you.

In the course of time you will merge with the dimensions of higher consciousness development.

You will merge with their colors and frequencies and with their distant worlds that are only a single step away. You will be able to approach the light beings that reside in those dimensions. These beings are already sending their light-filled signals into your reality and inviting you to enter their dimensions.

Your guardian angels and personal guides are already in contact with them; they communicate with each other and connect with you through loving vibrations.

The world of light and the light beings of the higher dimensions of consciousness are already waiting to connect with you. They are looking forward to welcoming you into their luminous realms.

Be aware that they love every one of you.

Every light being sees the purest light in you and looks forward to connecting with your light.

Detach yourselves from every thought that prevents you from ascending. Let go of thoughts that limit your possibilities. Let go of thoughts that keep you "down" and prevent you from thinking freely and light-heartedly.

Be certain that everything is possible in the time period you have now entered. You are no longer subject to limits and restrictions. Your mind has kept you trapped in the idea that ascension from the lower-vibrational realities is not possible—that is a thing of the past.

You are breaking down the structures.

Open yourself to new possibilities and allow everything into your life that seemed unimaginable or impossible yesterday. That is over.

Open yourself to the possibility that phenomena are now entering your life that you could not have imagined just minutes ago.

Open yourselves to all these possibilities.

Open yourselves to the possibility of phenomena entering your life that you have not even begun to imagine. Let go of all doubts that prevent you from opening yourselves to a new state of being and a new life.

Open yourselves to the new dimensions and spaces that are opening everywhere and that will bring you immeasurable happiness, joy, and harmony.

You are surrounded by an infinite number of beings who love you and accompany you. And these beings also include us, your Pleiadian companions.

> *We are with you, and we*
> *are accompanying you.*
> *Orella, Vilalata, Rahul, Milin,*
> *Wahou, Ramuel*
> *Peace with you. Peace with us!*

PART TWO

Messages from the
Pleiadians for the
Changing of the Time

1

You Are Kindling Your Soul Light and Finding Each Other

Sixth message from the Pleiadians for the New Era

channeled on 16 March 2022

Dear messengers of light!

You are close to your goal. The dark clouds are moving away and will soon disappear over the horizon.

Nevertheless, many people are still full of uncertainty about how this whole situation is going to develop. Many people have lost their equilibrium, their strength, and their confidence in a positive future. That is why we wish to make it very clear to you once again—and we will do so repeatedly: the positive future has already begun—the positive future in each and every one of you!

You have already come so far, and you have overcome great trials. Those of you who have passed these life tests and are moving on are the ones who are maintaining a stable energy on this planet. Do not give up on your positive plans and visions for the coming time period. You are close to your goal. So many dark extraterrestrial beings have already left your planet for good. Many dark beings were even happy to leave, because they knew that staying on Earth would only cause them more problems. Entire colonies of extraterrestrial allies have left your planet, taking with them vast, sprawling fields of destruction and dark magic.

Inconceivable things have also taken place underground, beneath your feet, all over the planet. But countless numbers of these hiding places and facilities have already been cleansed, and now the regeneration of the interior is taking place. We have installed devices in those empty, deserted corridors and rooms to help your planet purify and heal its ravaged interior. These devices increase the life energy in such underground rooms—rooms that were practically saturated with the horrifying energy of past times and the events that took place.

Together with our peace-loving extraterrestrial comrades, we have installed devices in the dimensions of Earth's interior that divert the accumulated emotions of horror, fear, and madness into other dimensions, where they are converted into light energy.

Nevertheless, it may happen that inhabitants of this planet, who carry similar, as yet unprocessed emotions within them, resonate with the energies that are currently being released deep within the planet and feel them in their own system of soul, mind, or body. In that case, illuminate yourselves. Go trustingly into your heart and bond with the Source, with your spiritual guides, or with us Pleiadians.

The regeneration phase of Earth's interior has already begun, and, once this phase is complete, we will move our technologies to the surface of the globe. We will then work there on clearing fields of negative emotions and manipulative emotions created by the dark beings and forces. We will cleanse and render these fields harmless too.

This cleansing is already helping many inhabitants to separate themselves more easily and effectively from the negative fields of manipulation and fear. Then everything positive, including a positive mood, will be able to spread even more quickly and easily. Many of Earth's inhabitants will receive new strength and hope and move on with renewed vigor. We know this because we have already started the work. And now, many of those inhabitants who do still choose to free themselves from the manipulative energies will have the opportunity to do so. The energy fields on this planet are regaining their clarity. The energy fields of human beings are being illuminated to an ever greater degree.

But be aware of this: many human beings have cooperated with extraterrestrial dark beings. It will therefore take some time before the old systems of manipulation and evil on this planet break down visibly. But the outdated systems will collapse and new systems will emerge on the basis of your higher consciousness.

It is important for you to know that we are with you. It is important for you to know that we are making every effort to ensure a smooth transition to the new systems. Go deeply into trust. Trust yourself. In this time period, flexibility is essential—flexibility in your actions and in your thinking. And you should bear in mind that a huge number of beings—both physical and luminous—are constantly helping you and accompanying you on your path during this time.

Realize that the occupation by dark extraterrestrial beings has lasted several thousand years. A holistic renewal cannot take place within a few months. Do not lose patience. You are not alone. Connect with your inner self. This will make you stronger.

And connect with other light messengers and light workers—for example every Monday from 9 p.m. to 9.20 p.m. in our joint meditation. That strengthens all of you. It strengthens your systems and it strengthens Mother Earth.

At the end of 2021, something wonderful happened that you should know about. Divine Intelligence activated the extraterrestrial peace-loving soul parts in those human beings who have come to Earth from other worlds. If you are reading this, you are one of those people. You would otherwise not be attracted to this information.

The activation of these soul parts awakens within you the memory of your light-filled task. It awakens the soul light within you. You are also one of those who kindle the soul light in all their systems and pass it on to those around them.

It will attract you to each other. You will then find each other more easily. You are creating a web of light that spans the entire planet, raising the vibration of the energy of the whole of humanity. You are raising the vibration of this planet through light energy that you have brought with you from your home planet.

Every one of you is important. Every single one of you. Illuminate yourselves. Consciously release your negative programs and let your light shine. It helps not only you but society as a whole. You are all connected. Everyone influences everyone else. Choose liberation and healing.

Liberation and healing begins in each one of you.

We are with you and accompanying you!

Your Pleiadian companions
Peace with you. Peace with us!

2

Increase the Light Vibration of Your Body Now

Seventh message from the Pleiadians for the New Era

channeled on 12 May 2022

Dear messengers of light!

We would like to give you some more information about the energetic processes that are currently taking place on planet Earth. These energetic processes have a great influence on the entire human community and, of course, on each and every one of you.

The new, increased influx of cosmic Christ energy that took place in April brings with it another great wave of purification of various systems of the human community. Many systems that are not built on pure thoughts and on the purity of their supporting energy will not be sustainable. Financial systems that are not based on purity are also slowly but surely beginning to fall apart.

On this planet, countless processes, affecting the systems of the human community, are already taking place in the background alongside or outside of you, as it were. There, in the background, human beings and other beings are already prepared to take up their task of building systems in pure energy and systems without manipulation. Many human beings and other beings have long since established new, pure systems in the background and are just waiting for the right moment to implement them.

The continuing influx of cosmic energy will result in interpersonal relationships being put to the test and brought to light. It will be even more easy to distinguish between those who are pure of heart and those who are still on the path of purification. It will be apparent whether someone has already allowed the divine truth to enter their heart. It will be apparent whether someone truly feels and lives divine truth and the purest divine energy and love.

Those who carry divine purity and love within them are protected by the purest divine frequencies. The human heart is the key to receiving and passing on divine truth and purity. The Christ energy, which has increased on planet Earth to a greater extent than ever before, is focusing on purifying human matter and preparing it to enter new dimensions that have already been made ready for you by Divine Intelligence. This entry into new dimensions will take place through a shift in space and time. All it takes is a tiny shift in space and time and you will find yourselves in 5D. Human beings who decide to enter new dimensions will undergo an absolute purification of physical matter to enable their system to bear the high-vibrational light of those higher dimensions.

Your connection with the purest frequencies of Christ light and Christ energy will help you to release the remaining negativities within your human systems and purify your body, allowing it to transition into these new spaces without difficulty. Your pure heart is the key to entering these new, pure spaces. Thanks to the light-filled, high-vibrational Christ energy, your senses are also becoming increasingly more subtle and are returning to their intrinsic natural state. Thanks to the cosmic Christ energy, your clairvoyance, clairaudience, and clairsentience are resuming their original function to the highest degree.

You will certainly notice a variety of changes happening in your body during this time and realize that your perception is also changing.

You may notice that you need more sleep or, conversely, less sleep than before.

You may notice that you are sometimes more tired and other times feel a great surge of energy within you.

You may also notice that your body changes its mass and that your weight changes from day to day. Your body currently needs a certain weight—sometimes more, sometimes less—in order to successfully release encoded negativities without energetic losses.

You may notice that your body craves food that makes it vibrate with light. It craves light, fresh, and blessed food. Therefore, bless your food. Blessing increases the vibration of your food.

You may notice that you are finding it easier and easier to communicate with your body, and that your body understands you to an ever greater degree. Your body has its own intrinsic energy and is connected with the purest divine laws and with the divine order. That is why it is sending you more signals and information during this time; signals and information that your soul and your mind—your intellect—are well able to understand.

You will notice that mutual communication between body, soul, and mind is indispensable for successfully stepping out of 3D reality.

Together with your soul and your mind, your body wishes to ascend into higher spaces and will therefore keep giving you the information needed to do so. Learn to listen to it. Give it rest and bless it. And the cosmic Christ energy that permeates your system will help you achieve your purest vibration in soul, mind, and body.

———

If you wish, you can use the following affirmation to raise the light vibration of your body. It is positively programmed with light, and every single word is connected with the field of higher consciousness.

Affirmation for Raising the Light Vibration of Your Body

And this is the affirmation . . .

"Now and in this space, I contact the intelligence of my body.

Now and in this space, I contact the energy and purity of the cosmic love of Christ.

Here and now, I ask my beloved body to absorb the cosmic Christ love, Christ energy, and Christ purity.

The cosmic Christ love, Christ energy, and Christ purity flows into every cell of my body.

In the here and now, every cell of my beloved body activates its inner crystal sun.

My body and all its systems are fully connected with the purest frequencies and with the purest order of the Divine Source.

I bless my body.

I bless myself on all levels of my being. I bless my existence.

Thank you, thank you, thank you."

We thank you all for your valuable and helpful energy work. We thank you for your existence here on this planet. You are on a good path.

We are with you and accompanying you!

Your Pleiadian companions
Peace with you. Peace with us!

3

You Are Just Learning What Unconditional Love Feels Like

Eighth message from the Pleiadians for the New Era

channeled on 9 August 2022

Dear messengers of light!

We greet you again from our heights and from our dimensions. We bring you words and frequencies of comfort, gratitude, love, and perseverance for this most significant era of all time for humanity.

Every one of our words that allows you to feel the vibration and frequency of our luminous dimensions of consciousness brings you a wave of light that illuminates your organism, your soul, and your mind. Every contact that takes place between us allows your heart and your consciousness to shine for at least the duration of this contact.

Every contact that has taken place between us up until now, whether through words or energetically, has connected you with our luminous, loving dimensions and with our vibrations of love. Every contact that has taken place between us has raised your light vibration and the frequency of joy and happiness in your cells.

Joy and happiness are the divine essence of your cells.

With every encounter that has taken place between us, we brought you a wave of the higher dimensions of consciousness to remind your soul of its greatness and light. With each encounter, your soul remembered more of its divine vibration, color, love, and origin. With each encounter, the seed of light, hope, and joy for the new, golden future sprouted more strongly in your heart.

Our encounters, our common contacts, have led to many of you remembering and through this ridding yourselves of the dark veils that were hindering your further spiritual development.

Every one of you is going through a significant time, a significant incarnation, and a significant development. Every single one of you. Everyone!

Even though for many of you your personal steps and the steps of the human community seem infinitesimal—possibly small and insignificant, so that you think you are hardly making any progress at all—you are all taking your own personal steps and your steps as a human community at a tremendously high speed.

We know that, from your point of view, this development seems very slow. But that is only because you are still bound by the quantity called time.

From our point of view, we clearly recognize that your personal development and the development of humanity as a whole is proceeding incredibly quickly!

Within just two years, millions of people have remembered their soul light during this exciting key time—millions of people who had never once before thought about their soul light and their divine origin. This special time has awakened in them the memory of the truth, and the knowledge of what and who is imbued with light-filled frequencies.

Open your hearts even further, because with an open heart you will recognize those human beings and other beings who vibrate at the same frequency of light as you.

You will then feel that you are not alone. There are already a great many of you! This we can confirm. From our point of view, you are like shining stars that have chosen a light-filled existence on this planet.

You are lights of the universe. You are star seeds!

Keep faith and remember that there are already a great many of you. Remember this whenever you feel that your actions are not producing adequate results. It is a fact: there are a great many of you!

The third and fifth dimensions of consciousness are still overlapping. You may notice that you sometimes lose your sense of earthly time. You may often observe that time seems to speed up or slow down. When you look at what is happening around you, it may sometimes seem unreal. You may then have the feeling that you don't belong, that you are just a spectator.

At such moments, you are practically on the border between 3D and 5D. You then stand in the middle of the interface and perceive both dimensions and realities in rapid alternation. As a result, these realities will look more clear-cut to you than before. In this way, you can learn to perceive what the different realities feel like.

You are relearning the subtle perception you lost to a great extent in past times.

Your perception will increase. You will also notice that you frequently see sparks or flashes of light. These are the lights of your light beings who bring you the light of their home dimensions and communicate their presence to you in this way.

You can now feel more clearly than before what true love, unconditional love, feels like, what love between human beings feels like, as well as love that flows to you from the light world. All this shows that you are becoming more subtle, becoming true human beings—beings of love and joy, beings of the fifth dimension.

And at the same time, in your world, behind the scenes, new systems are forming. Groups of people are coming together who are prepared to work on innovations for the new human community. Many have already gone public and are pointing the human community in the right direction, step by step.

Focus on what is essential for you.

Every single one of you: focus on the true, on the divine, and on what makes you human—new, awakened human beings of the new world.

And now we would like to give you an affirmation positively programmed by us to support you on this path. It connects every one of you with your divine essence. It binds every one of you to everything divine that you carry within you and that is around you.

Affirmation for Your Connection with the Divine

Say the following words out loud . . .

"My heart is filled with divine love.
My heart is filled with divine light.
My heart is filled with divine truth.
My heart is filled with divine freedom.
I am a child of the universe.
I am a child of light.
I am a child of love.
I am the purest divine essence."

And now say your first name out loud three times in a row. Your name connects you with your overall energy and your full power, which you brought with you from the Divine Source for this incarnation.

We are with you and accompanying you!

Your Pleiadian companions
Peace with you. Peace with us!

4

This Time Is Unique and Evolutionary for Every One of You

Ninth message from the Pleiadians for the New Era

channeled on 10 November 2022

Dear messengers of light!

We greet you from our luminous planes and bring you new and joyous information on planetary development—news that you have long been waiting for.

This time period is unique and evolutionary for every one of you.

Right now, human DNA strands are undergoing increased activation.

The rays of the sun are activating your DNA with their crystal energy, preparing you for the arrival of peace-loving star races and communities who have long been preparing for their arrival on this planet. Civilizations and communities in Earth's interior are also preparing for the arrival of these star peoples. You have all been waiting for this for so long.

With the arrival of these civilizations, the human being's perception and consciousness will increase. You are now being prepared for this more fully, and cosmic frequencies are helping you. Human DNA is changing its structure and becoming crystalline. At the same time, the human soul is experiencing light-filled expansion and is connecting with equally luminous worlds and spaces that are permeated with the divine information of the cosmos.

Civilizations and communities in Earth's interior are also connecting with human civilization on the frequency level and sending signals with information about their existence. Human beings are receiving this information and experiencing it in the form of strengthening frequencies, full of trust in the coming time.

These civilizations have existed in Earth's interior for millennia and are now preparing to come to the surface at the right time to connect their consciousness and information with you human beings.

But there are not only civilizations and communities in Earth's interior. There are also light beings there who are responsible for the human community. They exchange information with the beings of the cosmos—information on how they can best help humanity and its development.

Human beings sense that light beings are more present than ever.

Human beings sense that light beings are fully supporting and guiding them.

Human beings sense that the frequency of trust, which flows to them continuously, is helping them to transition into the positive time period.

Human beings sense that they are being supported by an infinite number of light beings, by their ancestors, and by their cosmic family.

After thousands of years of manipulation, human beings are beginning to feel a connection with the surrounding world of this galaxy. They feel a close bond with others of good will and with other beings from luminous spheres.

Human beings sense that the positive power of the collective is bringing positive progress and development for the overall situation of humanity.

The sustaining force of the positive timeline of humanity is constantly increasing. More and more people are joining this positive timeline.

These are people who have remembered their essence and have decided to leave the artificially created timeline of the negative past, once and for all.

One person after the other is stepping out of the negative, low-vibrational time period and switching to the timeline of the light-filled axis.

And human beings are developing their consciousness every day. They are developing at an astonishing speed. The human mind is freeing itself from the space of artificially created reality.

Everything is happening at breathtaking speed, and an unprecedented number of people are remembering. People are remembering—and the Cosmic Council is delighted at this development.

For although the human community has been helped from behind the scenes by peace-loving star peoples and light beings, every person must take the steps needed to liberate their own mind and liberate their own emotions themselves, without outside help.

Light beings from the cosmos and from within Earth are reminding each individual of their light-filled, divine origin. They do this incessantly. They help each individual, of their own free will and to free themselves, through their own strength, from the lower-vibrational levels.

We are very grateful that such a huge number of human beings are freeing themselves from the artificially created matrix and connecting their consciousness with the spaces of higher consciousness. This means that the intelligence of higher consciousness is spreading into the spaces and times of planet Earth.

Everything is going according to the plan of the Cosmic Council. Everything is going even faster than we, the Pleiadians, had expected. Those who have already developed their consciousness can feel how true our words are. Those people sense that a powerful, previously invisible force is guiding them and giving them support and the energy to act and liberate themselves.

Those people know that they will receive clear confirmation that their path is right when they connect with their heart.

We are grateful for each and every one of you. We are grateful for the light you carry within you.

We are grateful that, with your light, you are liberating your own existence on Earth as well as the existence of the entire planet Earth.

We thank you for your love.

Your Pleiadian companions
Peace with you. Peace with us!

My Afterword

Dear reader!

I am very happy to be able to accompany you—through my books with Pleiadian messages and exercises—on your earthly path, for this time brings great changes, not only in terms of the development of our community, but also in terms of its structures. And these changes affect each and every one of us. Before our incarnation on this planet, we chose this time period and this space. We decided to further the progress and development of our consciousness, and each one of us can confirm the changes that are taking place both outwardly and inwardly.

We have never before experienced this level of consciousness development—brought about by countless contributing situations and events—with such intensity in any of our incarnations here on Earth.

Everything is happening incredibly quickly.

Even if the situations we are experiencing in the here and now often come thick and fast, we still feel, in the depths of our soul, that light beings are accompanying us and that an invisible force is giving us the courage to carry on. In the depths of our soul, we sense that this power is also giving us confidence in our actions and confidence in the changes that are taking place in our environment and within ourselves.

Everything that has brought us to this stage of our development has been accompanied by a huge surge of cosmic light, cosmic love, and cosmic freedom.

You have probably already noticed how many people around us are reacting to the changes; and they are reacting very differently. Some are in despair, some are calm, some—those with an idea of the bigger picture—are even full of joyful anticipation. But it is true for everyone that, at this moment in time, we are rebuilding from scratch. Old, dysfunctional systems that no longer serve the good are disintegrating and new systems are emerging. For an incredibly long time, which many of us estimate to be several thousand years, human beings have been paralyzed and have experienced stagnation, the eternal return of the same old thing. Finally, sparks of light of divine guidance are beginning to come to life within us and our higher consciousness is taking the lead.

Now is the time for our consciousness to unfold and connect with the consciousness of other people—people who vibrate at the same frequency as we do. Our personal power is increasing and our personal light is visibly expanding. The lighter and freer our heart becomes, the lighter and freer our mind's thoughts become.

We feel that our pure intention is becoming increasingly easy to maintain and is gaining in intensity. We observe how our thoughts are connecting with people who resonate with them and how everything is manifesting more quickly. Our thoughts are gaining immeasurable, cosmic power!

At this time, the Pleiadians are calling on us to connect our thoughts with the thoughts of others of good will. They are calling on us to utilize the power of the human collective. I was also called upon by the Pleiadians to inspire more positive changes than ever before. I have been called to reach out to as many people as possible who, with their purest intention and through the power of the collective, can work for the positive future of humanity.

The Pleiadians have told me that, with just nine thousand people working with the same positive intention, a quantum leap could be made in the collective field of humanity, which would have a positive influence on humanity's development. And this collective work was to take place in October 2022, I was told, because the cosmic planetary constellation would be particularly favorable for it at that point.

I had conversations with my publisher about the Pleiadians' intention of achieving a collective impact with the help of as many people as possible. And lo and behold, there was already a large energetic field of love—created by the participants of the Online Channeling Congress, which has been taking place regularly for several years—on which we could build. And the timing was perfect, as the Online Channeling Congress 2022 was due to start on 22 October. We organized an opening livestream with me, to take place on that day, which we wanted as many people as possible to take part in. I am infinitely grateful that everyone I spoke to was as enthusiastic about the Pleiadians' surprising action as I was. All of us involved in organizing this important spiritual work were looking forward to seeing so many people work together energetically for the duration of the meditation. And we trusted that it would be successful, because the Pleiadians had told me it would. We trusted that this was exactly the right time to support the quantum leap in humanity's consciousness through the common heart power of the collective.

The Pleiadian beings always act in consultation with the Cosmic Council and only with its permission. They do not have the right to intervene in the affairs of humankind if it is not in accordance with divine law. But because the human community and the human soul, the human mind, and the human body had been manipulated for thousands of years, the Cosmic Council gave the Pleiadians permission—just as it had previously given them permission to accompany human beings and to assist them in their current development.

It was the first time I had felt such a strong and deep sense that we would manage to accomplish this great spiritual work. The organizers and I decided to ask the light world and its beings to support our joint effort. Shortly before the opening live-stream event, we all came together online and asked our ancestors, our cosmic families, and anyone who could help us for blessings. We asked for all spaces, times, and dimensions necessary for the quantum leap to be illuminated. We asked for support, and we connected with Divine Intelligence and with the frequency of cosmic freedom.

And then came the moment when all the participants joined the opening live-stream event via various digital channels. The transmission had begun.

I could not see on the screen of my PC how many people were connecting.

I could not see how many people were sitting in front of their own screens and how many were interacting with us in silence and without a digital connection.

When the meditation was over, I linked up with the channeling congress team and my publisher. We could see from the access data that there had been over 11,000 people! And that only referred to the number of linked devices and did not take into account the fact that more people may have been sitting in front of a single screen!

I think that, in addition to the more than 11,000 people, there were probably several thousand more who were also working with us intensively. This meant that we had far exceeded the critical mass of enlightened human hearts required for this energetic work.

I was so glad that the "mission" had succeeded!

The number of people who are simply doing light-filled work through their essence and their meditation is growing very quickly. Perhaps some of you reading this were present at the broadcast and also felt the magnificent, positive power of the collective.

Thank you very much for that!

The collective field of humanity is now radiant. It has connected with the radiance and colors of the universe. The light of the collective field has spread and the consciousness information it contains is reaching an increasing number of those who are searching. Because we are all connected with each other, many people are now managing, step by step, to remember their luminous essence.

We all suspect and sense that there are further major events awaiting us. We feel that these events are so close that we can almost touch them. When these events occur, it will be as if a positive timeline is separating from a negative timeline, as if there are two worlds, two realities that are moving further and further apart. And that will also affect the people around us. I can sense more clearly than ever which people I have a good relationship with and, by contrast, which people are distancing themselves from me without there ever having been any disagreement. Conversely, I can feel how an energetic, light-filled bond is growing between those of us who attract each other, which strengthens and nourishes us energetically. When people grow apart, I observe how invisible threads between them break and can no longer be reconnected. I feel no sadness or any other emotions. I feel that this is the way it should be and that things are taking their natural course. We all have the right to decide on the path we wish to take and the people we wish to meet along the way.

I know that everything has a purpose. I am sure you feel the same, dear readers. You feel that some stages of life are coming to an end and that new stages of life are beginning, allowing us to experience new adventures in a new time.

—

Last spring, I had an interesting experience in my everyday life. I don't remember that day being anything special. All I know is that it happened around Easter, a time when our beloved planet is filled with cosmic Christ love and Christ energy.

I was sitting at dinner with my partner and suddenly saw huge ethereal crystal rings moving through my kitchen. It almost looked as if they were made of cut crystal glass. However, they were completely transparent. So I could see through them. They moved through my kitchen, connecting with each other, connecting with my body and with my partner's body.

We had no physical perceptions when these luminous, crystalline rings were in our bodies. There was nothing to feel. But I could see that where our body matter appeared to be behind part of a ring it was no longer visible—even though the rings were transparent and subtle.

The phenomenon lasted for about ten minutes. During this time, I tried to touch the light rings. I succeeded, and I had the impression that the circular formations were pleased that I was making contact with them. It was simply magnificent, a wonderful light-filled spectacle!

I knew immediately that these rings were Pleiadian light beings visiting us. They sometimes take on geometric shapes when they enter our earthly time period. Circular shapes or forms such as those of mandalas are very typical for them. And then these crystalline Pleiadians informed me that it had to do with an important contact with their ninth dimension of consciousness. They told me that, through their "visit," they had connected me with other fields of consciousness and information that I should pass on to humanity. It had involved an increase in consciousness activity between the Pleiadian beings, myself, and my family.

The Pleiadian beings had brought me light-filled information from their worlds. Through this, they had expanded my ability to gain additional information from worlds to which I previously had no access.

This experience once again confirms their words when they said that information from the light world always comes to us in circles and that it is up to us whether we decode all the information of the "gift" at once or take a certain amount of time to decode it because we first need to understand or realize something else.

As we see, this time is full of magic and constantly has something new in store for us. But I love everything new, even if this newness arrives with enormous speed in these challenging times.

I also often need time to understand all the correlations in the information the Pleiadians give me. No one has become used to this speed yet. We are learning that information from the light world reaches us faster than the speed of light.

New things are constantly arriving.

Within certain low-vibrational dimensions and spaces, many invisible boundaries have fallen. Many boundaries no longer exist. Light beings can now approach us much more easily. And we them.

Another incident may serve as an example . . .

One day at a seminar, luminous cosmic doctors and healers contacted the participants. That was a great honor, because the seminar was about training future healers. The light beings descended from the world of cosmic magic into our earthly space and honored us with their visit, which was almost tangible. They told us that the participants in the group were included in the register of cosmic doctors and healers. If they needed help with healing, these cosmic doctors and healers would be happy to come to their aid. They said they had once lived here on Earth. They had worked here with the aim of helping people—and now they work from the light-filled heights and support everyone who has chosen to help and heal.

Anyone needing help who is acting out of a pure heart and with pure intention can ask for their support. All you have to do is "knock" on the door of the register of cosmic doctors and healers. Anyone can ask them for support. It does not matter whether that person works as a doctor or a healer or not.

I found the following information also very interesting: They told me that they work together with the light beings of the Cosmic Healing Pharmacy and help them with the selection and dosage of light-filled preparations for human beings who have asked for support.

This was another piece of the mosaic, helping me to understand that, for us human beings, the presence of the Cosmic Healing Pharmacy is far greater and more tangible than I had previously assumed. I had received the first messages about the Healing Pharmacy in 2021 for *Light Messages from the Pleiades*. The following year I received more information concerning the magnitude of this cosmic database to which we all have access. And since then, I have been receiving further messages about it from time to time.

Cosmic doctors and healers work hand in hand with ascended masters because they were once incarnated on planet Earth and therefore have a good understanding of us human beings and our systems of soul, mind, and body. I am firmly convinced that these cosmic doctors and healers will give us much more information on how we can help our systems.

The time is ripe for new information. The time is ripe to discover even more connections, ones that have so far been kept secret or hidden from us.

In the meantime, civilizations that have been living beneath the surface of this planet for thousands of years, such as the original inhabitants of Earth or the civilizations of the Lemurians and Atlanteans, are also making themselves known to human beings.

They are now contacting us again and giving us indications and evidence of their existence. They send impulses to us to further open the spaces of our perception and allow even more information into our minds, information that allows us to shine.

But it is not just we human beings who are shining and connecting with the light of our galaxy. An incredible number of light beings from within Earth are also connecting with light beings from the cosmic world. Many spiritual teachers are talking about how these light beings are sending us signs of their existence once again. We are now able to perceive them. They come forward with indications that will bring about a change in our ideas, our thinking, and our convictions.

I am firmly convinced that the information we will receive is already entering the reality space of humanity. It is already about to enter the minds of quite a few people who until now have lived in the conviction that what they see and observe around them is their true reality.

We are being prepared, step by step, at the speed at which we are able to absorb and carry it all. Everyone for themselves.

Dear readers, before I say goodbye to you for now I would like to pass on a message that reached me shortly before I finished this book. It comes from my great-grandfather, whom I unfortunately never got to know physically in this incarnation. He died long before I arrived on this planet. But you liked his message for *Pleiadian Soul Healing* so much that many of you wanted to hear from him again. He has contacted me once more and asked me to pass on this message to you as well. I am delighted to share his new message from heaven with you . . .

My dear great-granddaughter,
The purpose and goal of incarnations on Earth is to become and remain a good person. Of course, you will experience many diffi-culties and challenges in your life. But the important thing is to be pure and good at heart despite all the adversity and misfortune. Unfortunately, people who become embittered because of their

difficulties, and who look at the world with a clouded view for the rest of their lives, do not succeed in this task. They will most probably incarnate on Earth again, perhaps many more times. If you understand everything and live the love in your heart, even though you have often been hurt, then you have been successful.

People should become pure, light beings who do no harm to anyone and who can forgive. That is your purpose and goal on Earth. What you experience is just an illusion. It is actually just made up of pictures that are sent to you. And because people use a brain, they believe it to be their true reality.

Time is also just an illusion. It exists on Earth as a moving energetic constant that rules over everything and everyone. But its power is limited.

Love, on the other hand, is the all-conquering intelligent force. It radiates a wonderful and never-ending warmth. It is omnipotent from the very beginning. That is why love and the good always triumph and evil always perishes.

The more you understand the rules of life, the more love you will find within yourselves. And when you radiate this love, it connects you with cosmic love. As a result, divine cosmic love spreads even further, into all the spaces of infinity.

The rules here in the dimension of light are different to those on Earth. For us, there is no physical matter. For us, matter is just ballast. For us, only love exists in its purest form, as a beautiful and never-ending warmth. Here, we all appreciate one another. The all-pervading love feels like a constant hugging of one another. Imagine this wonderful and warming feeling in your chest and in your heart!

The thought form of information also functions differently here. All thoughts are connected, and we can all make use of them. But we only make use of them when necessary. For traveling in space and time, for example. The mere thought of the intention is enough to bring us to the place and time we wish to visit.

We are connected to the pre-eminent universal intelligence and can read the thoughts held in this intelligent form at any time.

And we are happy to pass them on—for example, to you human beings. Because thoughts are not our property. Thoughts are there for everyone.

We live here in the dimension of light, above all in the emotions of love, peace, happiness, harmony, and joy. We join with these emotions and employ them for the good. We use them to help others!

As a young man, I was constantly trying to learn more about Egypt because the mysteries of Egypt attracted me so much. Back then, it was not possible for most people to travel easily. They had neither the means nor the money. My greatest dream was to uncover the secrets beneath the pyramids on the Giza plateau and to connect with the spirit of the long-gone extraterrestrial civilizations that had worked in Egypt. Back then, I could at least travel to Egypt in my mind. I often said to myself: "One day you will get to Egypt."

And now, in this form, here in the luminous dimension, I can be in Egypt or in any of the other places that attracted me throughout my life whenever I like. I only have to think it. I can also be in several places at the same time. I can be on several planets at the same time. I can even be in different dimensions, spaces, and times at the same time. Here there are no limits. For us, there is nothing here that does not exist. We only need to think it and it is there for us. Divine Intelligence connects us with everything and everyone the moment we wish it. Divine Intelligence enables the multidimensionality of our being.

I would never have imagined in my lifetime that life in the light would be so grandiose and fantastic. I would never have imagined in my lifetime that I would one day exist without limits and restrictions. I would never have dreamed that one day I would have access to the database of cosmic information, which was created in light and love, and which serves all beings in this infinite universe.

Of course, times are changing for you and what we were unable to access on planet Earth in the last century is now available to you. It is available to all beings of good will. Whether in a physical or a subtle body. At that time, during my last incarnation on Earth, there were still many dark veils between the dimensions, spaces, and times that prevented access to cosmic knowledge. Now the systems of planet Earth are changing. The task of planet Earth is changing.

Planet Earth is returning to her proper order.

And the more love there is on Earth, the more love finds its way from you to us, and the more opportunities we have here to transfer this love and its boundless expression to earthly human beings and all other beings who are searching for love.

Realize that every pure and loving thought created on planet Earth also reaches family members who have already left their physical body. Realize that it is the same with each one of your emotions. And all of us here are happy to pass on these pure, loving thoughts and emotions to those who need them. We are all connected, and we support each other.

Thank you, my great-granddaughter, for your love and interest in me, for your love for other beings and for this world. Your love connects us all, across all dimensions.

It connects us more and more. Every day our connection grows stronger because every day your heart radiates more love.

Do not forget your own self. Do not forget that the love that grows within you every day needs space and time. Love connects us.

I send you my light-filled greetings.

Your loving great-grandpa
František Tejnor

And with that, I say goodbye to you once more, dear reader. I remain connected with you in my heart.

Thank you for your friendship. Thank you for your love and your connectedness.

From heart to heart!
Pavlina

APPENDICES

Message for the Peace Festival

Organized by Alicia Kusumitra in June 2022

Dear messengers of light!

We greet you from the starry heights and are able to bring you joy, courage, and confidence.

We are connected with your light beings, with your loved ones in the heaven of human beings, and with your ancestors. We are connected with your cosmic families who are watching over you and continuously sending you the frequency and vibration of the home planet you came from. We are connected with all your luminous helpers.

In your present incarnation you live on planet Earth, this beautiful blue planet. You have chosen to incarnate on this planet and you have chosen to help it in its ascension and to support the ascension of humanity at the same time.

You chose this task in the cosmic heights. You are noble, loving beings. Your light companions send you their love and thanks for your decision to help the planet and humanity.

You belong to the star seeds that spread the light of their hearts and the love of their souls over this planet. With your presence here on Earth, you illuminate your families, your friends, and your surroundings.

Every one of you is important. Every single one of you.

Even if it may seem to you that your help for this world is negligible—it is not.

Your light and your love expand, multiply, and connect with the light and love of other people of good will.

Your help for this planet is indispensable and important. Every day, you shine your personal light through the collective field of humanity, raising its collective consciousness. The energy of light and love on this planet is physically measurable, and the Cosmic Council measures the energetic field that surrounds your planet, brought about through the work of human beings of good will.

This world still needs a certain amount of your light and love to ensure that the physical value of the collective field remains unchanging and is able to connect with the higher levels of light and with light beings.

You are on a good path. Stay in your good will.

Stay in the light of your heart.

You are the star seeds that are writing a new chronicle of humanity on this planet. A new, true, genuine, and unadulterated chronicle.

Through your work, you are bringing light to your personal life here on this planet, as well as to the lives of your children and other future children who are already preparing for their incarnation on this planet.

When you stop at some point and look back on what you have done for this world, you will be able to say with confidence that your actions have brought about a positive change.

Stay on your path, stay in your trust.

Your heart's light will continue to connect you with us and with other light beings. We are connected, and we are one.

We bless your existence.

We bless your life and being on this planet.

Peace with you, peace with us!

Your Pleiadian companions

Message from the Pleiadian Beings Concerning the Year of Manifestation 2023

Dear light workers!

The New Year has begun on planet Earth and many of you are wondering what this New Year that awaits you will be like. How things will turn out and whether it will be as turbulent as the last few months have been.

We don't see the different periods of time in the way you do, and we don't count them in years. We perceive time as energetic chapters. We perceive their energy, their frequency, and color, their vibration and the vibrational rate of these frequencies. We perceive the vibrational energy of Earth's magnetic fields. On Earth's surface and inside your Earth.

But of course we know that time is divided for you into years, months, weeks, and days. This is how it was introduced to you by beings alien to Earth who do not think benevolently, and this is what the human community will continue to conform to until you ascend into higher realms of consciousness.

We would therefore now like to describe the time period that, for you, is the year 2023, divided into several energetic phases: In the first phase of the New Year, Earth's surface will increase its vibration. In the following phase, Earth's interior will increase its vibration. And in the third energetic phase, there will be major transformation processes that people of good will have been waiting for and looking forward to for a long time.

There will be changes that will bring people and nations together into a cohesive community. There will also be people and nations who will separate themselves from this community and enter into alliances that have no interest in developing further, neither in general terms nor in terms of consciousness. In a way, this will be the first noticeable separation within the physical worlds. In the course of time—but this will take a few more of your years—the worlds of these communities will also separate on the subtle level. This will also apply to political and economic organizations, which were previously of great importance.

We call the entire period of time that you consider to be your year 2023 the "Year of Manifestation," the manifestation of your thoughts, and the manifestation of projects that you may have been working on for a long time. Angels and light beings were sent to Earth for the purpose of manifestation, to help human beings use their thoughts in a targeted way so that they can reach their desired goal.

Your thoughts will become more visible than ever before. You will be able to see who is carrying low-vibrational thoughts and who is carrying high-vibrational, colorful thoughts. High-vibrational thoughts will quicken and will connect at the "speed of light" with the worlds and thoughts of others who vibrate at the same frequency. The thoughts of these people will resonate with those of others and there will be a mutual attraction between them. This will give them the opportunity to find each other and join in creating new systems and new structures or projects.

People will be naturally attracted to each other more and more in the near future—those who vibrate in the same way. And therefore, in the coming months of the New Year, these people will have a natural feeling for people who really belong together and those who don't, for people who strengthen each other through their interpersonal relationships and those who tend to harm each other instead. Many partners will intuitively and quite involuntarily sense whether their relationship is genuine or artificially maintained and actually only held together by everyday routines and habits.

The New Year will also bring you new and wonderfully colorful frequencies. Glorious lights will appear in your sky.

It will reflect the beauty of your galaxy and the beauty of the universe. Your Earth will communicate more and more with the planets of your solar system. Information from the sun for your healing and the regeneration of your DNA will flow to you even more intensively.

Formations will appear in your sky that you as conscious human beings will certainly recognize straightaway. You will realize that these formations do not come from your Earth. There will be growing evidence that peace-loving star races and their spaceships are accompanying you and are gradually preparing for their official arrival.

You will be able to observe spaceships time and again in their subtle form. Their subtle form allows them to travel to you with the help of luminous, subtle portals. Their subtle form will create the first energetic imprints for the physical arrival of these spaceships. These energetic imprints will provide a basis for initial communication with the human community. There are many physical spaceships already surrounding your planet. You have no idea how many there are. But they are still in inter-dimensional spaces, inaccessible to the human sense of sight.

And just as the New Year period will be full of changes, so you yourself will gain numerous insights in various areas of your life. It will lead to self-realization; to the discovery of your own strength and the power of thought; to getting to know the positive power of the collective; as well as to communion between people of good will.

Step by step, the human community is making more progress in its development than ever before.

This is now proceeding at a record-breaking pace.

Life situations and experiences will, it seems, happen at an uncontrollably fast rate, and yet everything will strive toward a rounded form.

Even if you cannot yet see this new, rounded form from your perspective, we can already see it very clearly. We perceive how the colored frequency of the human community is beginning to radiate in a variety of colors and how the energy is beginning to move in a circular form.

This is very good, positive news, because everything that is in divine order is made up of circles or circular forms, which, in your perception, can also create ring formations.

You may not be able to quite understand these words as yet. But nevertheless we can now tell you that the changes that have already taken place, that are taking place, and that will take place will bring you numerous positive developments and an expansion of the level of consciousness of your human community.

We are with you, and we are accompanying you.

We greet you from our time period and look forward to meeting you.

We wish you a wonderful New Year.

And we wish you a year full of trust, love, light, perseverance, and peace in your heart; and may you always be conscious of the company of your light beings, who love you unconditionally.

Peace with you, peace with us!

Your Pleiadian companions

Description of the Sun Symbol

We have programmed this symbol of healing for you and linked it with morphogenetic fields to help you connect with the natural matrix of the sun and the entire solar constellation. It also connects you with the energy and wisdom of the sun-soul, Ra, providing you with information concerning populated planets in your surroundings as well as their civilizations. The sun-soul, Ra, is the mediator between you and these civilizations in your constellation and your galaxy.

When you look at the sun symbol, your light chakras expand, enhancing your ability to travel to parallel worlds. The expansion of your light chakras enables you to connect more easily with every imaginable positive light being, in all spaces and dimensions.

At the same time, this symbol supports you in the healing and regeneration of your DNA, and in the purification of your pineal gland, a gateway to your higher consciousness. This activates your pineal gland to receive information from the light beings, facilitating contact during channeling.

How to work with this symbol . . .

It is enough to look at the sign of the sun-soul, Ra, to be connected with the sun of your constellation and all the possibilities we have described. Choose a period of time, intuitively, that seems appropriate to you. We recommend looking at this symbol for at least three minutes.

Description of the Earth Symbol

We have also programmed this symbol of healing for you and linked it to morphogenetic fields to help you connect with the earth-soul, Gaia, and all her frequencies. It connects you with your natural matrix system so that you fit back into the system of planet Earth. It also helps you to activate the light chakras under your feet, which receive Gaia's wisdom and information. They connect you with the meridians and crystal structures of Earth and provide you with access to the luminous dimensions that are located within Earth or are responsible for Earth's interior.

This symbol helps you connect with the purest order and the purest systems on Earth that Divine Intelligence has created. At the same time, it binds you to new, luminous systems of higher levels of Earth into which you are ascending, to divine systems without manipulation, and to systems that are free and perfect. It binds you to light information that flows to your planet and helps you successfully ascend to Earth's higher spaces. This symbol protects you with the power of Earth. It connects you with Earth and grounds you. You can use it before any energy work and before any channeling, but also after energy work and after channeling.

How to work with this symbol . . .

Just look at the symbol and you will be connected with Gaia and all the possibilities we have described. Choose the period of time intuitively. We recommend looking at this symbol for at least three minutes.

Acknowledgments

My heartfelt thanks go to all my Pleiadian and luminous companions who have accompanied me in the writing of what is now my ninth book of light messages from the Pleiades. Even though the time during which I wrote it was rather exciting and turbulent for all of us, thanks to my luminous companions I managed to write down their messages with astonishing ease, great joy, and within the time frame I had planned.

In moments like this, shortly after finishing a book, I realize again and again that the Pleiadian and luminous beings constantly provide me with the necessary strength, motivation, and time, without which it would not be possible for me to sit down with my notebook for countless hours to write down their individual messages.

At such moments, I realize that the Pleiadian and other luminous beings "provide" me with the time I need to sit down at my desk in peace and transfer their messages in electronic form to my PC.

At times like this, I have the feeling that the Pleiadians are "giving" me time for writing, as it were—or somehow extending it for me so that I can manage everything with ease between the many other activities that life as a healer presents me with.

Thank you all, dear readers, from the bottom of my heart and soul for your loyalty, for your support, for your trust, and simply for being you! ☺ ☺

I am well aware that our shared luminous field of consciousness could only develop so wonderfully into what it is today thanks to each and every one of you.

I am well aware that each and every one of you is an indispensable part of our collective community.

And I value each and every one of you. Your energy, your gratitude, and your connection are what motivate me and give me the strength to keep reconnecting so that I can receive the messages of the Pleiadian beings for you.

I also thank my family, I thank my partner, I thank my loved ones for their company and their heartfelt understanding that it is my mission to convey messages from Pleiadian and other light beings to human beings. ☺ ☺

Special thanks and heartfelt appreciation go to my daughter Nicole for her light-filled, loving translation of each word in this book into the German language, for the original German edition. I know that the Pleiadians love her for this and send her a huge amount of gratitude.

I would like to thank Michael Nagula, his partner Heike, and the whole team at German AMRA Verlag involved in the creation of the original edition of this book from the bottom of my heart. I know that they have all been pouring their boundless enthusiasm into this joint project.

I thank the Channeling Congress team for their love, their infinite diligence, and their perseverance in also bringing the messages of the Pleiadians and light beings that come through other mediums to the world of listeners and viewers.

⁓

I thank you all and send you a loving hug. Thank you, thank you, thank you for walking this light-filled path with us.

With love in my heart!
Your Pavlina

About Pavlina Klemm

Photo by Melanie Daoud

P AVLINA KLEMM was born in the Czech Republic, in the
Giant Mountains. At the age of nineteen she came to Munich,
where she still lives and works today. Even as a small child she had
contact with the light world and, as a young adult, the direction
in which her life's journey would take her became absolutely
clear. In 1999, shortly before the turning point of time, she began
working intensively with holistic healing methods. Working with
healing universal energy not only developed her healing abilities,
but also increased her connection with the light world and the
angelic realm. Thanks to this connection, she now sees it as her
greatest task to convey information concerning universal laws and
cosmic developments. Her channeling contacts with the Pleiadian
civilization has resulted in many books, CDs, and a card deck,
published in several languages, including the English editions

of *Light Messages from the Pleiades* and *Pleiadian Soul Healing* (Findhorn Press).

In her seminars Pavlina accompanies all participants in the spiritual development of their personality and trains them in Pleiadian healing techniques. She not only uses her skills as Lebens-Energie-Beraterin® (Life Energy Counselor) from her Körbler training and as a Reconnective Healing® Practitioner from her training with Eric Pearl, but also her training by Andrew Blake in quantum healing, and her training in Russian healing techniques.

Pavlina continues to devote herself to writing about cosmic laws, their complexity, and their direct influence on our human society because, as she says: "The teaching and recognition of universal laws is as infinite as the universe itself. It brings joy, awareness, peace, and purity to the heart."

For more information and current channelings visit:

https://pavlina-klemm.com

Also by Pavlina Klemm

Light Messages from the Pleiades
A New Matrix of Galactic Order

by Pavlina Klemm

*Pleiadian healing techniques to assist humanity
in the ascension process.*

IN THIS HIGH-VIBRATION BOOK, Pavlina Klemm shares
the light messages she has received from the higher beings known
as the Pleiadians on the Great Awakening that is taking place
worldwide. Included are exercises, affirmations, and meditations,
all charged by the Pleiadians with positive frequencies that activate
remembering and healing.

978-1-64411-825-2

FINDHORN PRESS

Life-Changing Books

Learn more about us and our books at

www.findhornpress.com

For information on the Findhorn Foundation:

www.findhorn.org

Scan the QR code and save 25% at InnerTraditions.com.
Browse over 2,000 titles on spirituality, the occult, ancient
mysteries, new science, holistic health, and natural medicine.